Travelli

A Book ot Days

Ann Murray

Cover: Reredos in Holy Family Church, Belfast.
Artist: George Walsh.
Photograph: Ann Murray.

I invite the reader to peruse *Travelling Light* in much the same way as one might take a walk along the shore, picking up curiosities now and then, while always taking in the bigger picture of beach, sea and sky. My intention in sharing my innermost thoughts is to celebrate my faith and communicate some of the joys of Christian living.

This publication would not be possible without the dedicated editorial input of my brother, John. His help and encouragement have been enormous. I am also greatly indebted to my daughter Bronagh who is responsible for layout and design.

The book is dedicated to my husband Hugh, my children Conor, Bronagh, Aidan, Kevin and Declan. Also my siblings, Mary, Gerald, Martin, John, Patricia, Pauline, Angela and Michael.

But most of all it is dedicated to my late parents, Patrick and Catherine, who in passing on the faith have passed on much more besides. May they rest in peace among God's angels and saints.

Ann Murray
December 2011

www.poetryprayerandpraise.blogspot.com

Renewal

Always we are being called
From what we know
From all that we regard as safe as home
From all that binds
Ancient hillsides
To ancient minds.

Always we are being called
To abandon boats and nets
And follow Him
On roads of buried landscapes
Paved with promise.

The Exaltation of The Cross

Over wounds it has triumphed
Over nails, and over thorns borne deep.
Through the ages it has triumphed
Through the long sleep
Of souls, of hearts turned cold
Of love spurned.

It has stood as the sign
Of love unshakeable
On the earth's most holy rood.
A rare profundity
Softens with each embrace.
Its centre flows out
Its veins to our veins, traced.

Let Out the Cry

Let out the cry
That struggles from beneath
The weight of sin.
Admit the yearning
That is buried deep within.

The voice that carries
Across a thousand hills
Carves the air
With a loving arc of wing.

Let out the cry
Let peace enter in.

Country Summer

Like haloes
The hills around us crown our days.
We bow beneath the leisured afternoons
And while away the hours
Like butterflies
Listing on bright flowers.

And when night falls
And steals from us the views
We find them still in tousled sleep
And vivid homeward dreams.

The Voice Within

It's not just from big works of literature or holy
books that we learn about Jesus. From heart to
heart moments we spend alone with him we find
a relationship that is gratifying and alive. God
teaches and instructs as much as our heart allows
during the course of our lives. Closeness to him
is less dependent on external sources and more
on openness and simple willingness to listen to
the voice within.

Rosary Meditation

The Rosary is Mary's gift to us - a gift of mysteries to her children. Just as her Son brought light to the world, the mysteries of the rosary permeate the darkness to bring light to the hidden corners of our lives. Mysteries of suffering, joy and glory are ours to meditate upon. We are uplifted, transported through time, brought beyond the boundaries of our own lives to the hill towns of Judah and the hill of Calvary; to the lowliest and holiest of places, and accompanied by Mary every step of the way.

Emmanuel, Emmanuel

To the man in prison, God is with us. To the woman sleeping under the railway bridge, God is with us. To the family struggling on a meagre income, God is with us. To the sick, the desperate, the lonely, God is with us.

Every pain of ours is shared by Jesus; every agony borne by the sinless one is our agony too. He knows the depth of human suffering, the anguish of desertion, the cruelty of blows. He knows the height from which souls fall; the dangers and temptations that prevail. But his message remains the same – God is with us.

Have no fear, raise your eyes as Jesus did, and look only to heaven. He sought light and comfort from his Father. Christmas is the coming alive, the incarnation of the beloved Son of God, born of Mary. Christmas is the time for the celebration of love. Not the love that hangs as a bauble on a tree and by January is gone. Not the love that promises us the sun, moon and stars and abandons us in a night. No. The love of God is an enduring love through thick and thin. Christmas is the joyful season of Jesus coming alive in us and for us - we walk as children born of light. We walk with God. God is with us.

Light of the World

You have come among us
Bearing light more brilliant
Than a thousand constellations.

Words of peace
Blossom on your lips
As light to the nations

Children race
To greet you;
We bow before the infant Christ
'Stay with us, little one, stay'.

Christmas Morning

To bless the morning
Is to receive it as a gift
And to unwrap
Its parcel of light
With openness of heart and mind.

Everything has a purpose;
The ribbons falling
Like rivulets of morning
From bales of sky
Connect us to the giver,
To the fingertips of God.

Joy, All Joy to the Earth!

Heaven is come to a humble stall
Light of nations, so small
We adore you in your nothingness
Sweet child of God.

Angels and shepherds are
Like swaddling clothes
Around you, Lord and Saviour;
Bind us to God.

Prince of Peace
We celebrate
Your coming on earth;
Your meeting us face to face
As God, as man
As child of virgin birth.

All light is in you.
All hope is in you.
Joy, all joy to the earth!

Hidden Graces

Like drawing water from
A well of darkness
We have no foreknowledge of grace
Nor eyes to see
The workings of God.

We journey onward
Hearts set not
On the perishables of this world
But on the promises of heaven

Trusting that in the world of the Spirit
Soul will penetrate soul
And together
We shall build the kingdom.

Fieldfare

Our cooks' hands stilled
By the unexpected -
A fieldfare visits on Christmas day.

Pecking at an apple segment in
A patch of cleared-away snow
It was in no hurry to
Regain its secret loft

But then
In a speckled flash;
It was gone!

It was a pleasing thought
That our garden was a wrought Eden
In the grip of winter chill;
And with the table tastily set
Our fieldfare ate its fill.

The Field of the Spirit

The field of the Spirit is brimming over with
good things. Stone walls have not height enough
to contain, nor mere intellect the power to
conceive of, all that is happening here.

Only Goodness himself knows
What is in store for the wise sower
As he leans upon the gateway
To eternity with God.

*"What a man sows, he reaps. If he sows in the
field of self-indulgence he will get a harvest of
corruption out of it; if he sows in the field of the
Spirit he will get from it a harvest of eternal
life."*

Galatians 6:7-8

Travelling Light

To not know what lies ahead is God's choice for us. Yet many people try desperately to see into the future. Goodness knows the present holds enough for us with its challenges, gifts, and beauty. The past is rightly in God's hands, forever put behind us. As we come to know God in the here and now, and grow in him, we throw ourselves more and more into the Divine mystery of His changelessness. God will provide. We place our hope in Him. And travel light.

Son of David, Have Pity On Me!

Luke 18:35-43

Serenity can be founded in human suffering, on a fearless plain, when seeing beyond sight brings the healing touch of Jesus to our lives. Not in a remote sense, but in reality we are touched by the master's hand and we are healed. We can see with eyes of faith, we can be free of burdens and we can alleviate the burdens of others through Christ working in us and through us. Our nothingness gives way to God's strength and power. God, when we let him, can permeate our lives with his loving wholesome self. There is no holding back. Just like the rays of the sun, God's grace pours forth upon us; he is the Divine physician with healing in his hands.

Waves

For Gráinne McCann

White-lipped creatures of the wind
That toss and kick and sin against the land
That saturate and spit and thrash and flay;
Repelling lovers with an evil spray
Of foam and chill that in one savage surge
Can strike a ledge like thunder
Dashing young to bits and earth asunder;
Then beat retreat to skulk into the night
Only to return again at dawning light…
…as gentle as a rocking chair in motion
As inviting as a turned down bed of ocean
Spewing frills and charm.

Brigid's Flame

Where paths of wisdom
And mountain learning meet
Brigid's flame burns on.
The light from
Cloistered listening
Glows still.

The veiled woman of history
Is the woman of today
Fired with zeal and
Compelled to share
The milled grain of the Word
As epiphany for souls.

To haul the hot coals of faith
To those in the scant margins
And to salve and balm the
Hungry prayer;
And the fear of raving madness
That shackles the lowly there.

Our Lady of Mount Carmel

Lovely flower of Mount Carmel
Fragranced treasure of God
The Jesus of infancy
Is safe in your arms.

The world and its riches
Can never compare
To all that you offer
In graces to share.

For all that is good
Stems from Love's gift given
And you in all sweetness
Are the flower of the heavens.

Too Often

Too often I've set out, only to turn back. Lord, give me the strength to keep moving forward, knowing that every step is advancement towards you.

"Nothing can come between us and the love of Christ, even if we are troubled or worried, or being persecuted, or lacking food or clothes, or being threatened or even attacked. These are the trials through which we triumph, by the power of him who loved us."

Romans 8:35-37

In My Heart's Deep

The narrow path rises before me
Hedges shoulder wintry grief
I repeat an aspiration in my heart's deep.

Guilty by desire,
Yet determined to follow through
This testing of belief,
That that which I cannot see
Is the essence of sweetness
That precedes and beckons me.

Adoration with Mary

I stand ready to place my hand in Mary's. She
waits with motherly patience to bring me to
Jesus. I close my eyes and picture in my mind
the roundness of the sacred host. I visualize an
impression of the face of Jesus on the bread. His
eyes are dark pools of sacredness that reflect the
midday sun as it dances on the water. I open my
eyes and look now at the monstrance with its
golden rays. Mary has helped me to focus on the
radiant beauty of her Son. In adoration we come
into the presence of God, himself a living spring.

Conversion

Imagine a field filled with wheat or corn, row upon row of stalks swaying in a summer breeze. Cereal crops do not appear overnight of course, but take time to grow and mature, and so it is with the health of our souls. We too need exposure to light. But more than this we need the nutrients that lead to growth; we need the grace and love of God. What a wonderful and blessed thing it is then to make the journey from darkness into light, to draw what we need from the well of God's goodness and mercy and to not look back. Just as death and burial in the tomb led to the glorious resurrection of Our Saviour, we too can be raised up as souls coming home, standing tall in fields of glory.

A Time for the Angels

Dawn is rife with light -
Among glistening thickets
And dew-laden leaf
Emerald brightness sings its rousing song

The world is awakened, shaken, renewed
Countless hosts are assembling
Throng upon throng

This is a time for the angels
For cohorts and legions
World-wide and day-long.

Adoration, Holy Family Parish

For Fr Gerard McCloskey

There is a place
For peace seekers,
A refuge for those in chains.

Between the shallows and the deep
Between grit and stores of grace
There is a place.

Pray that the Spirit will lead you there
Where fragrance sweet as children's prayer
Wafts heavenward.
Treasure more than gold
The peace you find
The grace, the beauty and the joy
That lifts the mind.

Then go to those you know
And acclaim with faith:
Friends, dearest friends,
There is a place....

The Body of Christ

If only society could replicate what is best about the church as a body. God's presence in the world is for me well characterised by his church-attending people. Judges, cleaners, teachers, car salesmen, painters, plumbers, musicians, accountants, health workers, long-term unemployed, sick, wealthy, troubled, blind – all come, all are living statements of his presence in the world and all are welcome in the house of God. He does not differentiate between our various walks of life, for it is the soul God sees, only the soul, and his heart is ever ready to listen attentively to his guests. We are like bright roses that float on the river of his knowing, stars that light his sky, for he loves us with a love that is full of mercy, yet full of mystery. If only our coming together in him, our witness in his church could be extended into all the areas of life, how different the world would be. With God's sight what would we not see, with his love what would we not accomplish, with his drawing power what factions would we not unite?

Annals of Time

The conference of trees
Beckons us
To a world of shadows.
We listen to their tall stories
As they resonate beyond the brook,
And into our very souls.

The tables turn and
Suddenly we are aware
Of fine-combing and refiner's fire.
The cowled brotherhood
Breathes on us
And records
The fingerprint
We have made
On the annals of time.

Prayer to Our Lady of Lourdes

Woman of God
Spouse of wind and fire
Freed from earthly desire
You lived a life of serenity
Under the shadow of the cross.

Placed among us at a point in time
And coming still
As woman bathed in light,
You see the world closing in
Awash with sin.

Your open arms are
Poised to deliver us from corruption
Into the arms of the merciful one.

Our names are on your lips like prayers
Yet the world is deaf to your pleading.
Save us, Mother,
Save us from ourselves

Heal us and pray
That the work of God begun in us
Will continue in the world
So that, sanctified and saved,
Over and over
We will be beautified by grace.

Heaven on Earth

When darkness comes and draws the veil on day
I will not despair of what is lost.
Should raiders come
And take away what's mine
I will survive

For deep inside
Is something of the heavens
That none can touch
Nor winter's season wither.

There dwells in me the ruler of the tides
I am God's and
We walk this world together.

Feeding the Flock

Today I will be the food
That will nourish another
By giving of myself.
I am doing what Jesus did:
I am feeding the flock.

Today I will be the
Easter water in the well
That will be drawn for others.
I will pledge allegiance
To the neighbourhood of God
Where saplings drink their fill
As each new morning
Spills upon the world
Its bowl of perfect light.

Watertop Farm

From the museum's chimney pots
Plumes of wood-smoke drift
Lazily across a summer-blue sky.
Swallows fly in and out
Of the opened doorway
Their white undersides
Tailed flashes across dark roof beams.
Near Cowslip Bridge
All that can be heard
Is a grasshopper in the undergrowth
And the symphony of water
Tumbling down grass-banked
Time-gouged crevasses.
Rare places and moments
Of beauty like this
Feed a knowing, an inner sight,
A correlation between
What the senses perceive
And the soul's hungry
Leanings towards light.

Living in God

If we don't love our God, don't walk his ways, then whose paths do we walk? Do we have total faith in ourselves, total confidence that we can do all things right, and achieve all we want by our own merits? Have we never known holy fear, or that depth of love and intimacy achieved through prayer that brings us momentarily to a higher plane and lifts the veil? If we don't love our God and walk his ways, we are not being true to ourselves. We are depriving our souls of light and walking in fog. We are not living life to the full if we are not living in God.

"Man Fully Alive is the Glory of God"

St. Irenaeus of Lyons
Early Doctor of the Church

I Thank You God for the Wonder of My Being

For Fr Colm McBride

Morning itself contains many of the wonders of God, when we see all around us the works of his hand through the lens of a new day's light. Peace prevails in such earliness - nature lends itself to an attitude of contemplativeness, when all that has value, all that is of God expresses itself in hue and in form, in height and in shallow, in beautiful landscapes of quiet praise.

Mindful that we ourselves in our diversity are made in his own image and likeness we can sense God's presence in our surroundings, in all manner of created things. The mysticism of the mountain does not in any way diminish the dignity of the little wren; the sound of a babbling stream cutting through green sward has power enough to call us like children to the lap of God. His greatness raises us to higher things; his meekness is the making of us.

"I thank you, Lord, for the wonder of my being."

Psalm 138: 14

Water-Bearers of Life

We are travellers
From a time that is not ours
To an eternity
Of God's design,

And as we bend like grasses
In compliance with his will
He smiles on us
His beauty in fingerings of softest light
His holiness not failing
His presence in
The water-bearers of life.

Japan March 2011

A wilderness of space
Nothing left to claim
Across vast devastated plains
Where lives once put down roots
And children's laughter rose
Like lotus shoots

Dirty debris-strewn streets
Are stored in pained
Pockets of the mind.
The forbidden fruits of fields
Once verdant, tilled and tamed,
Sullied now
And haunting as the grave.

The Thorns of God

Ingrained in knots of wood
Grief and pain co-mingle with precious loss
In suffering we are united with the cross.

Humbler then we proceed to journey on
As souls possessed;
Adorned with nothing and nothing other
Than the thorns of God.

St Joseph

A tender-hearted man of quiet depth
He walked blindly in pursuit
Of pillared truths.
He walked boldly
Where clouds of legions abound
And, wisely silent,
Stood staff to hand
Tenets of faith wrapped round.

August Gale

Clouds like horseless coaches career
Across the broken sky and
Branches heave and brush
Against the clearing air.
Birds use every trick
To keep their flight.
Cats pad carefully along
Wall-tops narrow and exposed
As every sweeping gust
Dead-heads another rose.

Divis Mountain

For Hugh

After twenty-seven years
We found ourselves alone again
On Divis Mountain

And something of God was revealed then
On our hearing
Lark song at invisible height.
A first for me;
It was a thrilling gift of the air
As clear and sweet as could be dreamt of
On a Belfast hillside.

Take Up Your Cross

We do not descend when we embrace the cross. We may taste the salt of our tears, we may stumble under the weight of its burden, and we may bleed as the rough wood bruises and blisters our skin, but always, we are raised up. We ascend to the plain where Love dwells and breathes holy fire upon the world; to the height from which Our Saviour gazed upon his mother and his friend; to the level at which all is changed through, with and in him. We rise above the confines of ourselves with all our weakness, sin and frailty, straight into the open arms of the loving God. We take up our cross and follow him.

"Then he called the crowd to him along with his disciples and said, 'If anyone would come after me, he must deny himself and take up his cross and follow me. For whoever wants to save his life will lose it, but whoever loses his life for me and for the gospel will save it...'"

Mark 8:34-35

Drawn to God

Drawn to God are rippling fields of fortune
Flush with horses that shake their misty manes
As hooves send primroses into random flight
Across vast thundering plains.

Drawn to God are souls, seekers in strife
Lost ones whose hearts ignite
With grace and fervour like thirsty-tongued sod
Quenched by the gentle rains of God.

While sweet-toned assemblies
Laud with song
The author of all living things
The form of beauty, order, day and night;
That through all draws all by His might.

Vessel of God's Grace

Mary shone in God's eyes
With purity none but the Spirit could
overshadow.
A grace-filled woman of Divine creation
A vessel of God's grace.
Achieving perfect balance between piercing
sorrows
And glorifying love and
Opening the window of our tomorrows
Through the workings of God and
The miracle of faith.

In Darkness and in Light

We never know what God is doing at any given time; or what the angels are about, or whose intercession in heaven has saved us this very day. So much remains unseen, but we can be sure that there is never a single moment of the day or night when heaven is at rest. The work of prayer and grace is endless; the effort of saving souls goes on and on; the communion of saints is a life line between earth and heaven, between that which we are and that which we would wish to become. And even when we sleep we are still in the presence of God while those on the other side of the world are rising, readying themselves for another day's work, believer and unbeliever in his sight, under the gaze of his merciful eye. We never know what God is doing but we can trust that all is unfolding as it should according to his holy will. We are his in darkness and in light.

Tide

Reveal to me, Lord
The purpose for this suffering today.
Enlighten my mind so I can see your way.
Help me to accept that you are on my side,
That all is gathered in the net
At ebb and flow of tide.

Showers

Someone yodelled above our heads and
The valleys played back the sound
As a river tumbles over rounded rocks,
Clean-faced as slate after a bout of rain.

A lone blackbird hopped
Among wild grasses wet and leaning
And the May morning of it all
Was sketched on a page of time
That memory would not erase
Nor a life time of showers fade.

Good Friday

A storm
Of dying
One greater than all of us
Nailed to a rustic rood

Head crowned
With starry briars
Torturous and crude

A kingdom mocked,
Spat upon,
Lanced through

Till water pours
Upon the darkened hour
A priestly dew
That meets the beads of mercy.

Letter to God

For Brian Monaghan

I will write to my God
On wings of vellum.
With the ink of well-water
I will tell of the things
That stir my soul.
I will praise him with the words
Of his own song.

Then I will set out for a lonesome shore
Or woodland, ancient and deep
And I will lift that love letter
Raise it like a cup.
And I will offer it to God
As a sacrament of the heart.

Birds will come at evening
Dipping their bills in fonts of stone
Where only the sun will decipher
The mirrored emblems of their flock.

And then in a moment
Born of beauty
We will rise
Homewards, and to the skies.

Countryside in Spring

For Fr Seán Cahill

The wild flowers waving from
Roadside verges are good deeds
And trailing smoke from the half-seen cottage
Is incensed prayer
The open window is a listening ear
To God, in the field of the hare.

The blackbird's song is fluted praise
And the moon the misted gaze
Of one who has surrendered thought
To miles of skies in beauty wrought.

The Best of Things

It does not matter that I am but a few yards from
the hustle and bustle of the street; it does not
matter what happened yesterday, or the day
before that; all that matters is the joy, joy, joy of
experiencing in the very depth of my being, and
in the marrow of my bones, the nearness of the
love of the Risen God. I don't deserve it but it
truly tastes good. It is the best of things, the
sweetest food of heaven.

Easter Poem 2011

He blamed not one nor sought reward
But that of doing the Father's will
And bore the weight of worldly sin
Upon his shoulder through the din.

Until on wood set on a hill
He gave his life that we might gain
A home above, a seat of rest
A place devoid of grief and pain.

But then in ways that scripture knew
There emerged a curious hue
The water rising in the well
The Risen Son the truth to tell.

His aspect changed but yet he walked
And ate and prayed with those he knew.
His wounded hands bore witness
To the few who grieved the loss
Of man and God, upon a cross.
And now in joy He is as one
With Spirit's fire as bright as sun
A risen Lord who holds command
Enthroned at God the Father's hand.

Death is conquered, light is come;
The dawn of ages is the Son.

Witness to the Gospel

Too many souls are living and dying without ever encountering God's goodness and grace. Too many are taking their own lives in what must be a mood of despair and utter hopelessness.

Faith and belief and trust in God do not make problems disappear, but enable the most weakened, hungry or endangered souls to see things in a new enlightened way. The gospel message is above all a message of hope.

We are to be witnesses - witnesses in the gospel hall of the family home; on the back streets and grey slab terraces; witnesses where mould spores grow on damp walls and beer bottles clog the drains; witnesses where there is pain and anguish and a terrible want in voices that rise from basements of human degradation.

Yes, we are called to be witnesses to the living God, to stand true to the gospel of life.

May 13th 2011

This evening at mass, just as the reader was reading from the Acts of the Apostles, I could hear through an open window a blackbird belting out a chorus for all it was worth. I could not help thinking that in some supernatural way that which was being voiced indoors, and that which was being sung outside, would intermingle so as to become one and rise like incense through the beautiful May air; on this the feast day of Our Lady of Fatima.

Dance of Freedom

I pray my soul will dance a dance of freedom
Where neither space nor calendar confine.
On air alone, and powered by heaven's virtues,
I will journey to the source of light divine.

I pray my soul will dance a dance of freedom
Rejoicing in the liberty of love
When glory and the transparency of grace
Will clothe me in the wonderment of God.

Letting Go

Let wings of prayer transcend the clouded skies
And carry voices to the gates of grace.
Let all the company of heaven
Hear our prayer.

Then trusting let us turn and go
Back to the life that's ours
And to the people of our time
And let them know
We place our trust in God

We love, and we let go.

Miracles of Grace

My body is your dwelling place O Lord. May
grace flow in me through channels of your
choosing. May my soul be as a landscape
window dazzled with morning glory, as light
penetrate its frame. And may the Holy Spirit
work in me true miracles of grace.

Slaughter without Cause

Too quietly it seems
The world is shouldering its grief
 Crying into pillows
Dark as landscapes from the fall
Dark as sorrows.
Too much outrageous liberty.
Too much slaughter without cause.

Milltown Cemetery

Two young girls
Diminutive beneath high Celtic crosses
Place fresh-cut flowers
On a bed of marble chippings
Cornered with cherubs,

Then straightening, they turn on their heels
And run from shadows
That crowd their sun
Chasing them
To places they are happier among.

Heart of Mercy

Her face is set like clay
Eyes as rubies raging in the fire.

Void of night
Let loose your stars
Set wide the gates of mercy.

Chilled dark, make way for
A pulsing heart;
An ear pressed to the wall
In readiness to hear
The first willed murmurings of prayer,
That rising, ragged-winged,
Take to the morning air.

Door to Door

For Maire McClean

These red-brick terraced streets
Are set in the hill town of Judah
And Zechariah and Elizabeth are
People of our time,

May wisdom be
As leaning branches
Above warm sills.

In visitation, may we
Bring God's light to hearts and homes
Among this holy land of streets
And rolling hills.

Our Lady and the Eucharist

When I think of the Blessed Trinity I cannot
ignore Mary for it was God the Father who
chose her to be the Mother of His Son through
the over-shadowing of the Spirit.

When I think of Jesus in the Eucharist I think too
of His mother who was there at Calvary and in

the upper room and when I think of the Holy Spirit I think of Mary his much loved spouse, and of Jesus' promise that he would send the Spirit to us as consoler and guide until the end of time.

And so in Eucharistic Adoration, in Marian devotion and in life in the Spirit we have constancy and the remedy for the ills of the world.

Soul by soul, light by light the darkness of sin can be rooted out. Day by day and prayer by prayer we each can be renewed. Brick by brick we can build the kingdom, one that shall not be destroyed.

"I saw in the night visions, and behold, with the clouds of heaven there came one like a son of man, and he came to the Ancient of Days and was presented before him. And to him was given dominion and glory and kingdom, that all peoples, nations, and languages should serve him; his dominion is an everlasting dominion, which shall not pass away, and his kingdom one that shall not be destroyed."

Daniel 7:13-14

Messenger

If man can train birds to fly across oceans and then to return home, how much better can the human heart be trained by God to listen to his Word, and carry the message of salvation to the ends of the earth?

Fruits of the Vine

The more conscious we become of the Blessed Trinity's in-dwelling in us the more we respect ourselves as bearers of love and bearers of heaven's light. In this sense material wealth loses its attraction, and the little gods of fame and power are like raindrops rolling off a leaf. True wealth and beauty is available to any one of us who reaches out to the Lord with a sincere heart. We can then become much more God-like and much less like ourselves, fruits of the vine bearing the dignity of the vine eternal.

Ascension

It seems like an ending
As well as a beginning
The going home of the Son and
The coming of the Spirit;
Like seasons changing, blending
Making all things new.

Heaven's gaze and grace showering
Our actions
Empowering with love
Enabling even greater things to be done
Than have already been seen.

Mercy's crowning
Of our belief.

Beds of Hay

The weight of a little one
Would scarcely dent such a bed
Yet the homeless, the dispossessed
Have nowhere to lay their heads
But beds of hay.

We know of a time
When God himself came small
And lay new-born in a stall.

Today
Near and far
The destitute ghosts walk -
Their eyes like lamps that
Probe the souls
Of us who turn away.

Can't you see us
On these beds of hay?
Can't you see him?
They say.

Mantra

A word or phrase that suddenly ignites
Inflames
Like roses caught in streams of light
Or candlelight trails
Fringing the edges of thought
Firing the mind with warmth.

Purest vision
That lines landscapes
Of the heart
With the silks of heaven.

Family in Faith

What good is it to receive into our souls the body and blood of Christ if we leave him there? Unless we then go out and bring that body and that blood to others we are defeating the purpose of the Eucharist. We are a family of believers, we gather in order to disperse, we multiply in order to divide, and our work is mission. To the ends of the earth we are called. We are God's witnesses, no less. The ends of the earth for us might be no further than our own home or place of work. We may see little change, we may hear of little difference but it is good to remember that seeds germinate underground. The hidden works of grace are as plentiful as fruit at harvest time, as numberless as stars.

Growing

We grow old only to be forever young,
We grow sick so as to enter the garden of olive
trees
We grow despondent so as to find hope in the
cross,
We grow blind only to see the light of Christ,
We grow unholy, only to be sanctified by grace
We grow poor of ourselves only to find treasure
within
We grow in the Spirit only to find peace in Him.

Portglenone Forest

No amount of words spread wide
Across this forest floor
No loose alphabets of leaf mould that endure
Could together form a liturgy of praise
As true to beauty
As bluebells in a May-time morning haze.

Trial of Love

If all my life's offerings result in just a fraction of a point of a thorn being withdrawn from the crown that mocks, the ring of pain that adorns the sacred head, it will be worthwhile; for through such things I partake in the intimacy of the wound, the trial of love.

Prayer to the Spirit

Holy Spirit, give voice to the silence in me. Let water flow across the arid landscape of my heart; let fire consume me so that I become a living flame of love, a light to others and an animated house of prayer.

Joy

True joy is like a door being thrown open so that the heart can run ahead into the fields of praise where the longing for awareness meets the closeness of God's gaze.

Billets Doux

The garden is filled
With the love-notes of God.
The patron saints of the bedraggled
Lie low under the bushes
Side by side with those
Of the bent-backed and the displaced.
So many messages are hidden here
About living and dying,
About beauty and care
About growth and resilience.
This garden of earth
Bears but a faint imprest
Of the riches that
Lie ahead for us,
In the Garden of Tender Care.

Acres to Explore

Sometimes in even the simplest of things like the way a leaf turns in a breeze, I find myself thinking of God. So much of what has been created points to him; flowers are like compasses that lead the heart to His Heart. Mountains are like the weather-beaten faces of nature that speak not only of times past but the future being rolled out before us, in paths to walk upon and acres to explore.

Invisibility

Tonight the sky is heavy with invisibility. What rolls, is rolling silently, what breathes is hidden under the canopy of night. I know that God exists, I believe in Him, in his presence and saving power. Yet sometimes it takes a night like this for me to realise my nothingness, to appreciate whose presence I am in, and to take up the offer of his giving of himself which feeds soul's hunger from within.

Field Of Blue

There is such deftness in the hands of God
Mysterious crafted workings that have shod
The foot as it walks on this glad earth and sod
There is such deftness in the hands of God.

On every stalk and rising golden grain
Are found inscriptions of the glory of his name;
On every sea the crested waves proclaim
A power that moves the soul and lights a flame.

Of faith that through the eyes finds proof to tell
His hands are craftsman's hands, He shapes the
bell
That hangs in steeple or in field made blue
By a thousand blossoms that of him ring true.

Milltown Cemetery Belfast

Milltown Cemetery is a place where Celtic crosses dominate the skyline and it is one of the city's oldest resting places. In the early May morning quietness I experienced a sense of equilibrium - a natural balance between the living and the dead, the gone before us and the not yet come.

Here is a place of peace and blessedness that in its own unique way seemed to bridge the gap between a sense of mortality and the hope of eternity, the air itself carrying on invisible wings the prayer that is whispered in many a heart: that those who died with Christ will rise with him on the last day, when every tear will be wiped away.

"They that sow in tears shall reap in joy."

Psalm 26

Lent

Lent leads us to Jesus. Our darkness needs God's light and our sin his forgiveness. By loosening our purse strings and giving to the needy we recognise our own neediness that takes the form of spiritual hunger. In lending an ear to God's word we may reflect on times when we listened but did not hear the cry in another human heart for love, for caress, for knowing. In prayer we come to appreciate our worth and dignity and strength that lies not in worldly things, but in the sacredness of the heart of God, the glory of his kingdom and the triumph of Easter.

The Settler

His capped head bowed under the leaking roof
of deep December.
His booted feet broke the tender
Skin that covered the bones of his world;
Whilst out on the fringe of the firs
Deer hooves ploughed
The snow beneath a sky-high ermine thatch
That sunlight would dismantle and dissolve.

He had listened to his heart
As much as to the tales of pilgrims
Before he had settled here.
It was his wish to live and write
And be there at the birth of new grass,
To step out beyond the swollen door
Into the thick of what matters.

The Shooting Lodge

He spoke of a grand house of black stone
And of how the Forestry Commission
Had come and paid a pound an acre
Only to raze the house to make way for planting.
I couldn't help but think of the stonemasons
Who once carried the dust from that house
Under their fingernails
In their nostrils
And ingrained on their very scalps.
And how much like love it must have been:
The workmanship, the art
The raising up;
The achievement in the taking part.

Beacons of Light

Sometimes I think I've journeyed far only to realise I'm barely off the starting blocks. God sends markers, doesn't he? They come in the shape of other people who help us gauge what stage we're at on our journey. Thank you, God, for these beacons of light who shine in our lives unknowingly, who become for us perfect examples of what we too can be, given willingness and grace.

Time

Only time will tell the whole story through that which has been written into our bones. Only time will let the scroll of who we really are unroll; for ours, like all history, is painstaking in the making, and enduring as the lived-in soul.

Ready

Nothing can prepare us for what lies ahead. The most beautiful flower in creation pales when compared to the face of Mary filled with grace. The highest mountain is nothing to the heights of ecstasy that the soul can attain; and the deepest ocean is shallowness itself compared to the fathomless depths of the sacredness of the heart of God. We cannot be prepared yet we can be ready to be open to the love of God. Ready to let grace work in us, ready to receive in the very core of our being all that Love is, and is willing to give so that we can be made new.

Home

Fly, spirit, fly.
Spread wide those wings of liberty
Soar high
Never stopping, nothing halting
Until you reach that place
Of mansions lined with mirrors
Reflecting light and grace.

Stay, spirit, stay
Among the chosen and the blessed
Rest, sprit, rest
With the known and the good

Pray, spirit pray
For those yet to come
That one day and forever
We will gather home from home.

Eucharist

In receiving the Lord we receive the goodness of heaven, for God alone is good and the Eucharist is food indeed. How well cared for are we who receive the body and blood of Christ, how well loved are we when we ponder his words: 'Do this in memory of me.'

There could be no finer act than that which replicates the action of the Lord at the Last Supper and when at mass we are gathered round that table as truly as if we were there in the room with him, sharing in the supper.

All of what is good; all that lifts up, all that heals and is merciful and loving is given to us in the body and blood of Christ. We can come no closer to him here on earth than when we eat the bread and drink the cup, for his body is food indeed, the strength that sustains us.

He has all we need for nourishment – the bread of life to beautify and fortify the soul is contained in His holy hands just as it was at the Last Supper and he waits ever-ready to help us rid the soul of all its impurities, thereby creating a fitting dwelling place for him alone, the Lord of life and Lord of all.

Anima Christi

In the agony of who he is, I am.
In the light of his glory I dwell.
In the joy of his rising
I raise my prayer
To heights that I cannot tell.

Into the abyss of mercy I plunge
And by the bones of suffering gain.
With the lamb I am the child
Bound on the altar of pain

At the banquet I am the solitary guest
Seated beside my Lord.
His body and blood as much in me
As I am in him absorbed.

Hand of God

It is not in our dreams that we are hurtling
helplessly down into the abyss and spiralling out
of control, but in real time. Was it not for the
hand of God coming to rescue us time and time
again we would indeed end up in the last place
we would think of going - and forever too.

72

Wisdom of God

The best possible way to see in a New Year is to be in step with God as we cross the threshold, in tune with him in our hearts and in union with him in purpose. Who can be fearful when God is hope, who can be anxious when God is at our side? When we are aware of God's love for us, his dwelling in us, we begin to love ourselves. To live in him is to share his vision, to see time as he sees it and to trust the future as we do the past, to his wisdom and love.

Easter of Our Lives

Too many Aprils have gone by
With hardly time for a prayer,
Too many dark acres hidden in the heart.

May my eyes be opened to the Cross of Calvary
That I might see no vile one hanging there

But one whose life was given up
Not for himself - for he was without sin -
But for the world
Out of dutiful love.

Such is our hope
That this one death upon a cross
Is of such worth
That all mankind
Can clutch its truth and say
'Yes, this is our Saviour
He is Lord
And this, this is His day!'

God is risen, faith revived
We too can celebrate and know
The truth and light
The hope for all
The Easter of our lives.

Darkest Knowing

When we begin to love God in earnest we place him centre-stage in our lives. He directs us like no other, and we learn more and more to tune our ears to that still small voice. It is the voice of authority and authenticity and yet it has a gentleness all its own. We learn to trust when we are established in his inimitable love. And it is this pure love that draws us beyond association and affiliation, right into the depths of darkest knowing, where we root ourselves body and soul in the Spirit's love.

Humility

There's something about the magnitude of God, that once grasped, helps us to understand His love – and how he loves us even though we may struggle to love ourselves. His love heals us of the guilt of our sins, thereby paving the path towards holiness and wholeness – a path that is bordered left and right by humility and a contrite heart.

The Room of the Sick

In the room of the sick we come to learn the value of the smallest smile, a sip of water taken, a remembered name – each is cause for celebration. Not proclaimed by the voice BUT enough to make bells ring in the heart. Life goes on....the sea is rough yet we are calmed by grace.

Beads

Many people have a fondness for a certain set of rosary beads. They may have been given as a keepsake from a pilgrimage or bequeathed as a treasured reminder of a parent or relative who has since passed on. Most people tend to kiss the cross and then before starting to pray the rosary, feed the beads through their fingers, letting them cascade from an upper to a lower hand as if enacting the flowing of grace. Each bead is symbolic of a droplet in a stream of mercy, a jewel in a crown of love, or a honed portion of the true cross to meditate upon.

Breath of Life

Enter in!
We say to the morning air.
Entice us to begin

The newest of new ways
By which to forge
A world made fresh
With the Word made flesh.

To come to truly know Him
And breathe Him into living.

Stranger on a Sunday

There bloomed in that dark tomb
A lily fair
That angels loosed upon the dawning air
Fragrancing the surrounding hills
With the scent of one of heaven

Then from a rock prised open
Time revealed
Rolled up garments....
Talk of a stranger in the fields.

Tree of Truth

The fronds of the world
Are dipping into pools of grace.
The pangs of hunger are satiated
By the bread of dawn.
The search for answers
Leads to the tree of truth
Bearing succulent mysterious fruit.

I must go to it
And sit
Under the holiness of its leaning branches
Where weightiness and light are one
Before the eye of the zenith sun.

Sea Shore

I went down to where the world meets the sea
Two friends well met it seemed to me
In and out of each other's pockets
Loitering, lingering, lovingly.

I went down to where the world meets the sea
And I could hear a battle raging
Enemies in each other's camps
And all guns blazing.

The Awakening

In the thickness of things
When nothing seemed that clear cut
The first whisperings were heard
Barely noticeable
Little nudges, gestures, words that
Seemed to take on a different hue
Like the way Spring sunlight dapples
A familiar view.

Slowly she began to listen more,
To realise
God wasn't somewhere yet unmapped,
Unreachable, in the skies.
No, He was in the here and now
Right there with her at home.
And as soon as she wakened to that thought
And welcomed the Good Guest in
The world around her sang with life
Each flower, each spoon, each room -
There wasn't a darkened corner
Or a place where joy couldn't light
For He was the heart's true Lover
And hers was a soul's delight.

Infant King

Mary sings her Magnificat
Like the psalmist at dawn
Hailing what the new day brings.

She holds close to her heart her beloved Son
And cradles our hope
For holiness in all things;
That we might glorify him
Who is our infant king.

Reminders

Night made perilous by a hundred swords
Any one of which
Could prove to be my stumbling block.
In vales of grief I tread
In pain aware of every care.
Revived by the sight
Rushing before my eyes,
Of things of hers;
Small and of little worth
Linens, beads, trifles made of wood.
And yet it seems that each has power to raise
To wailing pitch the sighs
The hidden pain
This walking on a bed of nails.

Dove

If I could know your name,
The name that heaven knows
I would savour
The sweetness of the sound of it
As it carries along our streets
As it helps heal
All the fragments
Of badness that litter
The open spaces.

All the desultory tones
Echoing in the alleyways of night
And in the ears of babes
All the blasphemous
Taunts that pose a threat
To peace and mar
The loveliness of our God-indwelling selves;
The beauty of who we are.

Come to me, Spirit of God

Come to me, Spirit of God,
Lean low to shelter this troubled soul
Comfort me for I have gone astray
And it is night
And I am far from home.

Come to me, Spirit of God
For you are love and guide
Someone's prayers have brought me here
For I am heaven's child

Come to me, Spirit of God
Let nothing mar your way
I surrender to you all that I am
Stay with me, Spirit, stay.

Clarity

Unless I see with the clarity of the Christ-eye
living in me, I will see people as the blind man
saw them – as trees, walking. Lord, remove from
my eyes all that blur my vision, all that keeps me
from recognising in the features of the other
person, your presence as light to the world.

Orchards

In the orchards of the Spirit
Every rooted thing bears the fragrance
Of the incense of prayer.
Every fruit and gift formed there
Hanging as on a thread from above
Invites us to taste
The sweetness of love

Trust In Him

Sometimes slow
Often fleeting
Time moves on

Only in God
Do we find
That which is unchanging

Even before his holy name
Was first uttered
In prayer, commandment,
Or even in blasphemy
God has remained the same

An inextinguishable flame burns
At the very centre of our lives
At the heart of all creation
And we are drawn to it
Like a bell that rings across a silent valley
Or a dulcet tone that reverberates
Down alleyways of misery
Through joyful mysteries and revelations
Through peace of mind or amid
The entanglements of turmoil
It encapsulates
The essence of His peace
His Love
His Divinity
And summons us as one.

As Roses

Sleep as roses sleep
Folded into night
Your worries and cares
Entrusted to God.

Hope in his love
Abandon yourself
To the darkness
That brings rest.
Awaken refreshed
Ready to receive
Blessings of light.
Limitless love.

River

How it goes
How it moves
Fast-flowing, purposeful
Like a thousand hooves
Thundering
Plundering with fright and fight
Tumbling and unstoppable
Whitening with light.

The Welcome

I have wandered
Far from the camp
Distanced myself from the fire
I have lost the gifted sense of direction.

But out there somewhere
There is a soul at prayer.
And somehow that dialogue
With God
Will have the power to turn my feet
And I will walk
To where he waits.
And he will run to greet me.

Joyful Living

Grace upon grace accumulates for the want of the asking and so, I humbly ask. I need God. I need all the graces He is willing to bestow on me, I need a life of prayer, a bed of rock on which to build my house. I have nothing that I can call my own, all is from Him.

Make of my soul a dwelling place, Lord. Furnish it with your love; enlighten my mind so that I may discern your will for me as I journey with you through life. Allow me to see in the littlest things the greatness of you. Banish from me all things that bring disgrace and all actions that bring dishonour to your holy name. Remove any unkindness that disfigures the face of love and casts long shadows over the brightness of joyful living.

The Healing Rose

Intimate as woven threads
Our prayers and hers

Her tears the beads we tell,
Her heart a home

Of mercy and of fire
That nourishes, consoles

Among life's pointed thorns
The healing rose.

The Ministering Of Angels

For Eileen McCormick

Along avenues of uncertainty it's not a case of
God jumping out at us but rather his shining a
gentle light into our darkness. Under tents of
despair when nothing seems good or worthwhile
a little bird can say enough to awaken the mystic
in the soul. In a period of anxiety the touch of
another human hand can be the touch of God,
the ministering of angels.

Something Happened

Something happened that changed everything. No-one knows precisely the hour, no-one witnessed who was there, but when the morning came, angels were seated on stones – what was sealed was open, what was inside was gone. It was the strangest thing – and it changed everything.

"Now on the first day of the week Mary Magdalene came early to the tomb, while it was still dark, and saw the stone already taken away from the tomb. And so she ran and came to Simon Peter, and to the other disciple whom Jesus loved, and said to them, 'They have taken away the Lord out of the tomb, and we do not know where they have laid Him. . .' and she beheld two angels in white sitting, one at the head, and one at the feet, where the body of Jesus had been lying."

John 20:1 – 2:12

Until the Appointed Hour

Until the appointed hour
Nothing can rent this
Thin veil of flesh.
The body remains a tent
Pitched on the pastures of earth
While a captive ear listens for liberty's bell;
Soul's flight to the gates
Where Christ himself waits
And all, precious all, will be well.

Supper

He came among them like one from another
country.
They did not know him – they who had known
him well. The talk was of strange happenings,
excitement and bewilderment. And they were
compelled to say 'Have supper with us, stay and
rest.' At table the stranger's face shone. And at
the breaking of bread they were one. The miracle
of him impressed -
their Lord, their master, and their guest.

There Is Always Hope

No matter where we are in this world, no matter what our circumstance, no matter how far removed from God we might judge ourselves to be, there is always work going on behind the scenes, there is always hope. Prayers rise like incense every minute, voices sing to God, adorers kneel before the Lord of Hosts and heaven hears earth's bells ringing. Whether prayer is coming from a hospital sick bed, from a small congregation gathered for morning Mass, or a monastery in the testing hours of night, all prayer is carried to the ear of God, to the heart of heaven. No-one can know for sure just who is receiving or will receive graces this day and just who, awake or asleep, is being fortified against the raging world as he or she is blessed by God, and enfolded in the mantle of love.

Mission

God is with us -
We are as islands
Draped with beauty others cannot see.
We look to heaven and pray
For graces to succeed in bringing Jesus
To hands that plead
To hearts that weep
And hunger for more than streets
To lean on in an hour of need.

In secret worlds
Wounds bleed
As feet onward plod
Smarting with pain
As real and wearing
As the wounds of God.

Healing

Love purified and love refined.
Poured over the gaping wound of another's sighs
As the wind stings the eyes that try to smile;
Bright as coins
Among rubble and plight.
Heart speaks to heart
In words decipherable only
In darkness's paragraphs of light.

Sun's Rays

I give thanks
For those movements of this day
That connected me with Jesus.

Word, deed or gesture
That produced a smile of joy
Or compassion witnessed from a place unseen.
All these were revelations to me
Of grace at work
In surprising ways
Affirming through the hours
God's healing through
The sun's rays.

"For you who fear my name, the sun of
righteousness will shine out with healing in its
rays; you will leap like calves going out to
pasture. You will trample on the wicked, who
will be like ashes under your feet on the day I am
preparing, says the Lord of Hosts."

Malachi 3:20-21

Gathering Spaces

For Rosaleen McGuinness

There are gathering spaces
Quiet places where kindred souls can meet
And offer a prayer.

Believing
That there is more unseen than seen
More taken up, than passed by

And heaven is closer than
The open door
To a morning full
Of promises
And sky.

Christ the King

We are heralds of the eternal king
All of us united in Him.

All in heaven and on earth is singing
For this is his time.

Calvary is the battlefield
Earth ruptures, new life begins.

The Risen one is light now
Countenance brighter than the sun;

Seated at the Father's hand
His rule is mercy, at love's command.

Garden Birds

For Hugh

He has an eye for them
Much more than I.

Lamenting their lack
With heavy sighs
He hungers for the gift of
Their morning surprise.

He has an eye for them
Much more than I.
His kindness a counter
To the savage sky.

Traditional Airs

Like elderberries gathered
In the aprons of the wind
To make wine for the music makers
Tunes are passed down from
Generation to generation and
Revered and respected as
Reliquaries of love.

Mercy

No fool is he.
No hiding place exists.
His is the all-seeing eye.

Yet his too the fountain of mercy
To which all can come;
For to exclude
Would be to put
His children in a place
Other than the hill of Calvary.

Here we come first
And his death comes slow
In all its brutal agony
And serves to show the lengths
He is prepared to go
For love of us.

No fool is he.
No hiding place exists.
Mercy flows
And all of us
Are His.
Receive the light.

Receive the light
For the hungry soul is
Not satisfied

With any other bread
Than that of life.

Accept the gift
Let grace ignite
The temple within.
Inflame your heart
Witness to the Word.

Music

For Fr Colin Crossey

We lift up our hearts.
The buried song resounds
Once more.
From ocean depths
To highest heaven
There soars
In silence, and in singing,
The voice of man
And earth's mute praises ringing.

Advent

There will come a day when each of us will be held accountable for our actions and our words. Every last penny that has passed through our hands will have to be accounted for. Any trust placed in us, any guardianship, stewardship, duty or responsibility will be examined in the light of the sun.

Advent is a good time for looking inward and putting things right in preparation for the fresh start of the New Year. Each Advent leads us to a new beginning with the coming of the Christ Child. It is through God that we will be truly enriched, as it is through God that all things will be made new.

Golden Words

'We'll see....' were the words we waited for
Enough to have us, the youngest advocates,
Turn on our heels and
Run to the prompters -
Older siblings
Who were waiting in the wings.

She said 'We'll see -
And that means yes!'
We blurted out

And suddenly
The heavens opened
And the room was filled with joy.

Psalm 41:13

Deep calls to deep in your rushing waters: and
all your torrents, all your waves
have flowed over me.

Deep calls to deep.
None can deny
Soul's affinity
To soul.

Deep calls to deep.
Beyond the shallows
Under rock and reef
Things sleep.

Deep calls to deep.
And all of heaven
Sings
At love's awakening.

Out of the depths of longing
Baptism is sweet.
Soul meets soul.
Deep calls to deep.

Psalm 62:127

I will take joy in the protection of your wings

Through lightning storm and gale
When I am weak and senses fail
When clamour without
Threatens the peace within
I will take joy in the protection of your wings.

When I grow weary of the race
And sense my soul devoid of grace
And I am bowed by the weight of sin
May I by grace the battle win
As I take joy in the protection of your wings.

When the moon is veiled with cloud
And no bright stars about her crowd
As winter trails its shawl of lace
Over treetops, hills and springs
To the rock of hope I'll cling,
I will take joy in the protection of your wings.

Gift of a New-born Child

Let this child be
A symbol of hope;
Her peaceful presence a ray of sunlight
Bursting through a canopy of leaves
To dapple-mark the earth
With irrepressible light.

Let this child be a source of
Endless joy;
May she be the sign in our lives
Of goodness
Beyond reckoning
And love beyond belief.

Mother Woman

Jewel by jewel
you garnish
a private memoir
and furnish an heirloom
set in whispered silver.

Loves and losses
triumph and travail
tell the burnished truth that
before you were a mother
you were a woman.

John McKeever 2011

That The World May Believe

There are people who have lost their way, souls that are far from God. Some are in the Church, others not. Some struggle with the darkness of addiction or temptation, some wander in the desert of illness or loneliness, others are ensnared in isolation due to psychological disorders and some are afflicted spiritually.

The more prayer and fasting offered up on their behalf, the more healing we will experience as one body. God in his wisdom sees and knows who is in most need of his mercy; and the best we can do is to aim to be generous in our praying as God is in his mercy.

Divine Mercy is God's call, but in his goodness and graciousness and generosity of heart, we, as adopted sons and daughters are invited to share in this great work by praying for souls, for our brothers and sisters, that they will see the error of their ways and come to know the healing touch of the Father's love.

"I pray not only for them, but also for those who will believe in me through their word, so that they may all be one, as you, Father, are in me and I in you, that they also may be in us, that the

world may believe that you sent me."

John 17:20-21

Woman at the window

Who are these ones I see
Moving nimbly in the fields
Heads high, like people unafraid?

Who are they that come
Past dusk
Carrying no light
Seeming not to stumble
Where the road is rough?

They move in unison
Yet I don't know what they do
It's as if they go about some work
And it forever new...

Feast of the Immaculate Conception 2010

O Mary conceived without sin
Chosen to bear God's only Son
You are more beautiful
Than our imaginings
More steadfast than ancient hillsides
Crowned with light.

Pray for us.

O Mary conceived without sin
Ark of the Covenant
You were
Immaculate from conception
And immaculate still as
Heaven's pure bouquet and
Queen of the angels.

Pray for us.

O Mary conceived without sin
Pearl of eastern light
Mystic sapphire of night
Shower us with heavenly graces
Guide us with gentleness.

Lead us home.

The Lilies of the Field

Considering the lilies of the field, I bring to God the cares of this day. I remember those who hunger, the grief–stricken and the dispossessed. I bring to him great hordes of unbelievers, as well as souls who have lost their way and others who are searching.

I remember too those selfless souls who go about doing good for God's sake. I bring the carefree and those who are dancing, rapturous with joy.

In coming before God I realize it is not in the big things that I can make a difference, but in the small. I will listen here for a while, and ask God to unite my prayer with the universal prayer of the Church that reaches heaven.

We are never alone. God loves us with an enduring love. In all our brokenness and ungratefulness we are still his beloved. In our joy he is joyful too and in our suffering we can choose to be at one with him, in every breath, even to the last.

"And why are you anxious about clothing?
Consider the lilies of the field, how they grow;
they neither toil nor spin..."
Matthew 6:28

To Not Be Afraid

To not be afraid of God
Yet to fear him
Knowing his justice
And loving his ways
Is to honor him
To invite him into our lives.

To adore him
Who is divine
Is to bow before him
And to not be afraid
To love as a child
To ask and to listen
All the days of our lives.

And I Shall Let You Go

When all familiar sounds begin to fade
Only then will it be heard
Carried on the air
Sweet as a bird's calling
In a larch at dawn.

And as you turn
To listen
Your heart will know
That it is more than song.
For notes are never dressed
As beautifully
Nor ears more filled
With such exquisiteness.

It will be then, my love,
That you will see
As through a veil dropped low
All that beckons you
To where you want to go
Is the beauty of the Lamb
Caught up
And brought low
The flame that melted hills
Of hardened snow -
And you will run to him
And I shall let you go.

At Home In Silence

God is at home in silence
In the depths of joyful mystery.

He communicates
With the soul
So as to share with us
The essence of his being
And cultivate within
A purity of heart
That is a mirror
Of himself;
A perfect leaven.

Obedience

The seal of obedience marked him
His life a round of goodness
That stood fast against prevailing winds
He knew the ins and outs of things
Could list the constellations
And listened to the trees
Swaying against the backdrop
Of his beloved hills

He knew every hedge in
The fourteen rows
That made up his walk
Returning him each nightfall
To a Calvary of sorts.

Garden

Working among the roses
Is his summer holiday.
Caught up in a flotilla
Of colours and scents
That transport him
To holy temples
He finds in
Exotic Edens
The fragrance of God.

Christ the Universal King

There is a golden thread that connects us to the source of God's glory. We do not always see the thread – sometimes it runs underground and we travel blind. But always a link remains between the Creator and his created ones, between the children of light and the Sovereign Lord, between the cross and the crown of glory that awaits the loyal subjects of the King of Kings.

Bread of Heaven

There is something of the radiance of God
That shines on hills in the morning
Then in a moment it is gone
Its fleeting nature
Speaks of need elsewhere
Of hungry eyes searching the dark beyond
Ravenous for the least morsel
To fill that emptiness which only God can fill
With the bread of heaven.

Summer Scene

An invisible runner is igniting patch after patch
of gorse on the hillside until it appears as a mass
of yellow flames. As far as the eye can see the
sun and the gorse flower are engaged in playful
rivalry.

Real Living

He had little time for books
And favoured more the reading of seas and
skies.
There was no doubt that he had chosen the joy
That gives rise to lilting and whistling
As he moved about his day.
He drew from within him notes
That coloured the world
And left for others
True patterns of reality.

Letting Go

She knew she was being taken
Where she did not want to go.
With all her pent frailty
She raged under a sky-blue counterpane
That defined her every bone.

And in the end,
When mustering did no good,
She curled into a sleep.
Like a beautiful leaf brought low,
And with neither fire nor frenzy,
She let go.

Poet

For John McKeever

He went out
Holding nothing
But a candle to the night.
And in the way
That a red-skinned apple
Surprises by the whiteness inside,
The darkness about him
Gave up its store of secrets, of juices,
Of underfoot mysteries.

On earthen floors
Under branches
Bending and unbending
He found a resonance
With his lonely soul;
A whispered eloquence
That left him hungry no more.

Prayer

To pray is to enter into a space apart where the mind is free to engage with God in openness and love. It is another dimension in which we imbibe the essence of God and this enables us to carry his holy fragrance back out into the world of work and leisure. The closer we grow to God the more the different dimensions merge until *all* our living becomes as prayer. All pure actions are borne to him on the wings of his own glory.

The Glory From Within

Even before the world takes on the matt of day
I am moved to praise.
Even before the dark-eyed flowers open to his
gaze
I am moved, by love alone, to praise.

I am stirred by a wind.
The voice of God amid the din
Speaks to my searching soul.
I am moved to praise
The glory from within.

I am moved to praise as angels praise,
As saints under that sinless lover's gaze
Blaze as flames of light. I ask of God
The grace to praise and praise
All that comes from him, all that comes
From heaven's height.

Christ the King

He sits on a throne of Irish oak,
Inscribed with Celtic scrolls,
About him flows a velvet cloak,
His crown is of purest gold.
His majesty and power are hailed
As choirs around him sing,
He whom we sinners scourged and nailed
Reigns high as King of Kings.

The Power of God

God knows
The reason for
The twist of orange
Round the lace hole
Of the seabird's marble eye.
He numbers
The fine cloud lines
That make up
A mackerel sky.
In His all-knowingness,
No mysteries exist;
There is no question-
Omnipotence is His.

A Time for Praise

There is one God,
One who loves and goes on loving
One whose love abounds.
He is here and near
As He once was yonder and hither,
He breathes life into the day
And warmth into the darkness.
His is the light that floods the heavens,
His strength is in the tides
And His mercy streams from age to age,
His is the voice of the bleating lamb,
The beauty of a hillside trapped in light,
The river in its rage;
There is a God
And now as ever is a time for praise.

Departed

Today I remember you.
I shall pen a song,
Give it wings
Then linger a while
And watch as it is carried out
Over the thunderous waves,
Up into the dark violets
Of this November sky;
And as I pray for your soul
I shall ask God in His mercy,
That when at your journey's end,
You will gaze upon His face
And be glorified in Him
Forever more.

Ballycastle Beach

On golden sand clean and wide
The children played for hours.
Later with crude, sharp-edged stones
They struck and hacked at
What they called the chipping rocks:
Two rugged, weathered basalt mounds,
One part-submerged, the other beached and
steady.
And as they worked to gain new holds
Or sat on top while sizing up the bay
It seemed the world was easy for the taking,
All that could be conquered in one day.

Glenariff Waterfall

To the right, high above our heads,
From glistening outcrops
Of rock and red earth,
Side by side with ferny foliage,
Steady trickles of water, thin as harp strings
Seeped into the ground below.
And to the left a torrent, which as it thundered
To new depths, downpoured unstoppable,
Elemental, white scattering light.

Christmas

1.
Joy

The bare-branched trees are beautiful
And winter skies sublime,
There is comfort in the coldness
Which heralds Christmas time:
In the starkness of a stable,
In the meekness of a birth
The Prince of Peace Incarnate
Brings joy to all the earth.

2.
Peace

May the light of the dawn
On that first Christmas morn
Stir hope in the hearts of men,
May the peace of Christ's birth
Restore to the earth
The will to bring war to an end.

Our Father

His hands reach out
And in our helplessness
He raises us
Till we can see
Beyond familiar hills
A kingdom sweet:
An eastern light revealed.
His love is ours
And all we have is His
Every breath we breathe
Every hour we give
We offer,
For in Him we live.

The Glensman

Son of a hill farmer,
Baptised in the river of Glendun,*
Reared in the faith of his father.
Naturally shy among men,
Nowhere more at home than
When taking the lonely road
Between Gruig Top and Crockaneal;
His only company bullfinches resting
On a hazel bush or grey-backs
Picking at bones by a watery edge.

Just past the Mass Rock
At Craigagh Wood
He claimed a seat of prayer,
Honed by merciless elements
Whole seasons had ensnared.
He lorded in the land
Of such rich heritage,
Yet was humbled always by
The thought that God for him
Was present in the Glens,
As sure as rock.

*Glendun (in Irish: Gleann Abhann Duinne) translates
into English as glen of the brown river and is one of the
nine Glens of Antrim in County Antrim.

126

St. Therese of Lisieux

Fragrant flowers and a picture
Tell a story all their own
Of how beauty thus created
Are God's, and God's alone.

Bonamargy Abbey

In the sheltered grounds of the old ruins
Grasses rise up between the tilted stones,
Ancient rough walls thinned by time
Now mostly stand alone.
Inscriptions hint at histories
Of service in God's name
Of cloistered halls and prayerfulness
And beeswax tongues of flame.

Portaferry

Three men are fishing from a boat moored
At the quayside where
Afternoon sun is dappling the north end
Of Strangford Lough.
Cormorants are resting on island rocks like
Stationed sentinels.
Inland, in the old castle's demesne
A dog is chasing swallows,
As raindrops dribble down
Switches of ash and holly.

Children are everywhere, delving
Their growing sun-tanned limbs
Into the corners of stretched-out days,
Their hearty laughter
And their called-out names diluted and
Diminished in the briny air,
Like songbirds besieged by rain.

We, the newly-fangled stop and stare at
What the locals have
Long since taken in:
The moods of the Lough,
Its wayward traits,
The ferryboat, the birds, the buoys,
The light at Ballyquentin Point,
The up-to-the-ear conch shell noise.

Newcastle, Co. Down

As shifting chiffon
Veils the grape-dark hills
And winding trails,
Night falls and stills
The restless branches
Of the forest trees
The angry mobbing
Of the worked-up sea.
As shifting chiffon
Veils the grape-dark hills
And winding trails,
Night falls and spills
Its liquid darkness
Onto Widows' Row
And sparkly starkness
On the pier below.
As shifting chiffon
Veils the grape-dark hills
And winding trails,
Night falls and fills
The sleeping children's heads
With seaside themes
Of kings and knights
And princesses,
Of castles built on dreams.

Tollymore Forest

Standing under a cedar of Lebanon
Was a prayerful experience
For I could not but think of God
Near the restful waters of the Shimna
With the backdrop of the Mournes;
And for a while at the Hermitage
There was no denying
The supernatural calm
Amid an all-round leafy loveliness,
Chapel-ed with tree-top psalms.

Questions and Answers

He moves barefoot through grass and reeds
One hand's sweep can scythe a field,
Some have asked if what I hear,
If what I see
Is real or plain imaginary.
The answer lies somewhere in the rain
That strings glass beads
On wires and frames
And springs the earth to life again
That it might yield fine barley.

Put Out Into the Deep

Put out into the deep
I will sustain you
Even while you sleep
My graces will contain you.

Put out into the deep
My stars will ever guide you,
Nothing shall you fear
I am there beside you.

Put out into the deep
Though stormy seas surround you
Steadfast work will reap
Catches to astound you.

The Sign of the Cross

There's talk of an imminent journey
Beyond the hill and the spire
They say it's a long and narrow road
And it leads to a paschal fire.
We're assured of a lamp to our feet and
Food for the hungry soul,
And the graces and joy of Easter
When we come to the crown of the road.

Evening

Moths lingered,
Their diaphanous wings
So penetrable
That it was possible to see
As through a silk screen
The colour of the geranium flowers
On the windowsill

Buds like bunched fingertips
Easing their grip
On the hand of day
Growing languid in the humid air,
Dipping their roots in indigo.

Coast and Glen

It's a sanctifying moment
When the soul's immersed and cleansed
By the ribbon of bright water
As it courses through the Glens.
To discover above Red Bay
Where the high cross stands at Layde
How the sandstone work of masons
Bears sound witness to their trade.
To see stubble left by balers,
Or pink fuchsia in a hedge,
A rooster by a farmyard gate
Or a guillemot on a ledge,
Instinctively protective
Of the egg clutch in the nest
Is to drink the cup of nature
And know it's heaven-blessed.

Becoming Light

For Fr Paddy McCafferty

He walked on silver plains,
Through light, becoming light,
Drawing others out of the dark
Rooms of their minds, embroidering
Their lives with the silken wings
Of his words; when little children ran
Up to him and stared into
The same eyes His soul looked of,
Wonder met praise.

Mary

Intuitiveness of a woman
Gracefulness of a lady
Pureness of a heavenly heart
Charitableness of an intercessor
Motherliness of one who listens
And waits, unable to settle
Until the sound of the key
In the latch marks the safe return
Of the wanderer to their eternal home.

Preacher

They say his tongue
Is a sliver of flint
As sharp as any implement
That fashions Irish oak
For palaces and kings.
But I say only this:
One evening long ago
When hidden and small and still
In the grass by the edge
Of a goat path,
I heard the lone bell
Of his voice
Carried downhill on
The shoulders of the wind,
And what was said
Was meant for none
This side of paradise.

St. Francis Xavier

Ships' timbers bore the tread marks of his feet
Beneath a looming, ever-changing sky.
Month after trying month of mission
Charting dark and turbulent waters,
His heart on fire,
Compelled by desire to bring God's love
To India and the Far East,
To baptise in the name of the Father
And of the Son
And of the Holy Spirit,
To bless the sick, the poor, the afflicted.
Finally, with mainland China in sight,
He was taken ill -
God's will perhaps that he should linger
Long enough to see a prize sunrise,
Its oriental brilliance kindly soft
On his now dimming eyes,
Yet right for his life's flowering.

Cushendun Beach

The hull of a white-sailed yacht
Is in line with the horizon
As a fisherman casts out
On an incoming tide.
A washed-up dog fish is turned backwards
And forwards by the motion of the water,
Its back slate-grey, its belly tide-white.
Gannets fly and dive, then swiftly
Regain height despite water-weighted wings.
Slender grasses sway in the sand dunes,
Behind is Rockport Lodge * – the poet's home
in the Glens.
Looking now I wonder which her favourite
window was,
Which light she wrote best by,
And of the little that has remained unaltered
here,
What most caught her eye.

*Home of Glens poet Moira O'Neill

Northern Foreshore

Reclamation would not be easy here
Without a fight, the sea has clearly
Defined its hold, marking these walls
Noxious green that slimes onto
Thicknesses of resistance.
You moved south where warmer winds
Rounded the corners of your Ulsterisms,
Yet it is to this same spot you return
Time and time again, your painter's
Eye scanning the coastline, your mallow
Cheeks ever-resinous with rain.

Derelict House in the Glens

Behind the roadside house
Lilac blossoms overhang the rocky burn,
Ivy branches imitate art form
In a contrivance of twists and turns.
Sedges, hawkweeds and nettles stand
Well past shoulder height,
Where grave-faced boards hide windows
Stone walls are a silver-trailed white.
In an air that is sweetened with heat
Blue and orange glow bright
As smoke drifts up from the chimney
And surrenders itself to the night,
Grouped voices of chattering children
Can be heard at the rise of the latch
As the door of the cottage opens
And the hands on the clock turn back.

Mary Ellen

On the evening before the ship sailed
She whispered a valediction
Into the ear of the wind -
Words not meant for the left behind,
And like a best friend
The wind blew westwards towards the sea
And scattered her words
Like bangles of roses on the waiting water.
Circles of cormorants and shags
Waked her leaving at first light
And watched us as we cried -
I and a Brent goose
With sand grains in its eyes.

His Sacred Heart

It was neither a petal-strewn path
Nor a mountain track that brought me here.
It was neither a blinding blizzard nor blistering
sun,
It was neither the dawn chorus nor the curlew's
call,
It was neither the rocky shore nor the open
fields,
It was neither the ancient woodlands
Nor the city throngs,
It was neither the boisterous sea
Nor the soughing wind.
No, dear Lord, it was none of these.
For it was love in its wholeness that brought me
here
And love and love alone that keeps me here
Where there is shelter and peacefulness,
Light through the night hours
And food for the soul.

The Cherry Trees

Always a source of disappointment,
How seemingly in an instant
The beautiful blossom is gone,
But the ground with its covering of
Pink snow
Consoles us for a time-
Though we have lived in pleasant
Shadows long enough
To know that off the tree
And after a night of rain
Each petal will shrivel and fade
And be lost to us again.

Cavehill, Easter 2003

For Harry Morgan

How beautiful the city looks from here
Gilded with an Easter morning light
A robin in a hedgerow shows no fear
While homing in on leftovers of night.
Church bells in the distance mark the day,
A fitting tribute to the risen Lord
Who by His crucifixion led the way
To truth and life by loss of His own blood.
Still, certain sadness fills the air,
Belfast bears its crosses long and tall
As history casts grey shadows down the hall
Of memories that darken and ensnare;
But Jesus in His dying shared our pain
And by His rising, raises us again.

Cavehill, historically known as Ben Madigan
(from Irish: *Binn Mhadagáin*), is a basaltic hill
overlooking the city of Belfast in Northern Ireland.

Easter Morning, Knocknacarry

For Charles McCormick

High above in branches limed with light
A blackbird sings on my behalf-
Something from the Book of Psalms
For the risen Christ, something
To delight the angels.
What is glory but man at his best?
The hunger I feel inside,
Just now, is put to rest.
In peaceful ways God hears my need
And through the songs of birds
He fills my soul with grace
And I am healed.
To speak with Him on mornings
Such as these is a window
Onto heaven through high trees.

Oh sing, blackbird, sing!
Fill these glens with music
And sweet praise
For Jesus Christ is risen
And darkness, like the stone,
Is rolled away.

Divine Mercy

When I hear of the worst imaginable crimes, the most heinous offences against Love, I must then look inwards. For it was for all sinners that Christ died on the Cross, and it is not for me to dwell on the sins of others, but rather to repent with true sorrow for personal sin, and then to rejoice in God's mercy, knowing that it was for a soul such as mine, that Jesus died and rose again that I might know Him and speak His Holy name.

Biding Time

In the little breaks
Between rambling words
You can hear her soul's yearning.
My trained ear
Has grown used to the
Heaving and moans of
Sea and northerly winds
In her spirit's wintering out.
And it is no coincidence
Now when she stands
At the door of spring
The prattle lessens
As the light advances in.

Mary

Like the branch to the tree inclines
Mary adhered
To God's will
Not once questioning
Or wavering
Or testing.
In obedience
She set up home
At the altar of God's love
And saw herself as handmaid,
As instrument.
And in offering all
She pleased her God.
Now, when we recount such love
And move to imitate in faith
She towards us inclines
With measures of God's grace.

Without End

Jesus came to call sinners. For me there's a certain consolation in being less than perfect, knowing that God loves me as I am and knowing He holds a special place for me in His heart. And He's not the sort to go pointing a finger, nor does He come across all high and mighty. In fact He does the opposite. He waits patiently for me to speak with Him, and then when I listen in the silence that follows I become like a child again, wrapped in the warm blanket of His love. Deep within my heart I know we are meant to go through this world together, He and I – there is no-one more willing to help me. In every situation, no matter how dire or complicated it may seem, He is there, my faithful listener and loving friend. So it has been since baptism, so it will be without end.

Mill Bay

The waters of the bay are lying low.
Grey seals are languishing on rocks,
Their bodies motionless under the sun.
Out beyond the shoreline
Oystercatchers have settled
On slippery spits, their bleeping
Shrill and loud in the breezeless air.

I am at rest, half asleep,
Swinging gently in a hammock
Of the mind's making,
Between dry land and the sea,
All sense of time forsaken,
All worries tossed to the side,
Airborne and willing to travel
Out of myself for a while.

The Parting

(In memory of Pope John Paul II)

This feeble heart
These trembling limbs
I offer to the King of Kings.

My faltering voice
No longer rings
But in my soul
It sings and sings.

When I close my eyes and dream
I wander by green fields and streams
And pick wild flowers
Where hills are steep
And breathe clean air
And breathe it deep.

One day these dreams
Will never end
And we will be as one again
And look upon the face of Love
And live in peace forever.

Fledglings

Unravelling woven intricacies
Of an abandoned nest
Finding fragments of speckled eggs
Rummaging later in the attic
For that old ornithological guide
Stumbling in the dimming light
Feeling something give beneath my feet
Discovering the broken hand
Of her first Christmas doll
Picking up fragments of wan porcelain
Cradling them in the folds of my palm.

Mercy

With a fatherly love I was welcomed -
A sinner who will sin no more,
With the help of heavenly graces
That abound round the heavenly door.

I asked for and was granted
More than I'd hoped through prayer-
A penitent's plea for mercy
From the Heart that lingered there.

The Living Day

I cannot hear the company of heaven sing
The cherubim and seraphim
Nor can I see the beatific face
Or visualise the queen resplendent in her robes
Nor move among the angels glorified
By God and grace and heavenly abode.

But I can house within my heart
A hope that lights the darkest night
And feeds the soul and leads me
Through the narrow gate

Along an arrowed way
Outward and onward
Into the living day.

The Master

When Jesus sat talking with James and John
As night edged in over ebbing waters,
Did His words hang in the humid air
Like grapes on invisible vines,
To be plucked and shared,
Savoured in a time when finer dust
Would trickle from their sandals,
And the unfamiliar stir longings
For brotherhood, for signs,
For reminders of the sense of homeliness
That marked a Jesus-centred Galilean night?

Rathlin Island

Westwards, past the harbour, buzzards soar
silently
Above hills of abounding heather.
Beyond the meadowsweet of marshland
And mallard of fresh water,
We reach, by rough road, the Bull Light.
Castellated sea stacks are nesting sites
For fulmars and kittiwakes,
Whose incessant soulful cries
Drown out the wash below.
An endless rancid rise of fish oils
Invades the nostrils,
While eyes and mind take in
The bastion that is the West Light,
Built with fearlessness and skills honed against
The hacking chillness of a might
That floored a thousand wrecks,
And hoarded bone on bone.
These islanders knew suffering:
The repeated bloodlust of invaders,
A people slaughtered almost to a man.
From Cnoc na Scridlin*, on stormy nights
A relentless sound of wailing
Is carried downhill by the wind
Lest the living should forget
An ancestry thinned to a bloodline
A heritage enshrined in island pride.

*Translation from Irish: Hill of the Screaming, a site of
infamous massacres in 1642 in which women and children
were thrown over cliffs to their deaths on the rocks below.*

Pockets Full of Stars

I've come upon him down bramble-walled lanes
And stood for the word or two he'd let loose
With a shift of his cap, before he'd pass me by.
His are solitary ways.
I've turned in time to see
Big radish-red hands
Work themselves into an awkward union
Up the Lenten slopes of his back
As he shies away westward
Into the Antrim hills
Darkness falling down around his shoulders
Like a great top-coat
With pockets full of stars
And locks of fox-red hair.
And never have I called him by his name,
And never has he looked me in the eye.

Surrender

Somewhere in the void
Of my nothingness
Waiting for the surrender
Of pride and vanity
And selfishness
Rests the bark stripped bare
The whittled-down
White-boned truth
Of what I really am
And all I desire to be:
Your servant, Lord.
Mould me, Lord.
Make me pliable,
Shape me to Your will,
Give me courage
And perseverance in Your sight
That I might lose everything,
And live to love You.

Ordinary, Everyday People

There are times when it's nice to be alone, even necessary to have some time out, but for the most part I benefit and grow by being in the company of others - those who would be classified as ordinary, everyday people. If you were to look at them, I doubt you would be struck by any particular characteristic, yet it is these individuals who conceal about their person absolute gems - riches of wisdom and goodness, humour, patience and joyfulness - fruits of the Holy Spirit.

The Blanket

It smells of Tuesdays after school,
Columbo and Fifteen-to-One,
Buttered toast and tea with sugar,
And at least two biscuits on the side.

It smells of TV and puzzles,
Tangram and Patience,
And guessing which hand holds
The larger half of the Opalfruits packet.

It smells of laughter
As they untangle a misunderstanding
Over the 'dark' man or the 'dart' man,
And she waves him away, wordless in her mirth.

It smells of warmth and quiet
Photos looking on from the mantelpiece.
He is there now in his garden
But I can still hear him lilting.

It smells of a happy greeting,
"Hello, Bronagh!"
And a shuffle in her chair to see me better,
And a tug of the blanket across her knees.

It smells of stories of Tyrone
And people long passed,

With interruptions as I am made to take
At least two biscuits
from her "stash" and one more for home.

The woollen blanket, red and green
Worn every day since I made it
Is mine again – a gift returned.
It smells of them
And wraps me in different
Sort of warmth.

Bronagh Murray 2011

At Your Feet

I could bring you flowers, dear Lord,
And place them here by your feet
And someone kind will arrange them in a vase
And others will come and pray
Long after I have gone away.
But today it is I who comes
With empty hands and open heart
And it is I who will stay at your feet
And in the quiet listen to your words:
More beautiful than the language of flowers
More silent than the silence of the hour
More welcome than any earthly sound.

Poem for a New-born Child

Let them build no walls around you, little one,
Look on the world as home.
Walk barefoot if you wish, tread dew,
Let them build no walls around you.
Scale peaks, sail seas, seek out the true
Casting falsehoods into sloughs of foam,
Let them build no walls around you, little one,
Look on the world as home.

All Along

About an hour into the walk the sun disappeared behind some pearly clouds, but I was undeterred. The undulating hills still beckoned, the heather still sang its lovely purple song and it seemed just then the world toiled not. What was shaken out of the aprons of last year's winds was now firmly rooted underfoot and every nook and cranny teemed with flower and life. In the distance I could see a lone figure on the crest of a hill, stick in hand, and I immediately thought of my father. Hours of days spent gazing into the distance, his eyes fixed on something far, his blackthorn stick pressed deep into the turf, like a needle stuck in a groove of dreams. It's a grand day, he would say, and then he would whistle or lilt for a moment or two before drifting back to where he was heading all along.

My Light and My Life

Dear Lord you are my light,
And my life.
To waken at the break of day
And know you are there
Invisible to the eye
Untraceable to the finger
In the silent lifting mist
Loving me with divine love
Transforming me by grace
How can I not respond
With praise and praise and praise?

Bright Stars

Children can, and often do inspire. Yet they
manage to do so in the least sensational of ways.
No big speeches, no dramas, no essays, no
monologues. Quite often all it takes is one
spontaneous, forgiving or loving word or gesture
on the part of a child to turn a tense situation
right round. While we adults may consider
ourselves superior, on many occasions it is the
children of this world who shine like bright stars.

My God and King

I have seen my God and king
In those who have no home
And He has walked the path with me
When I have walked alone
And in the silence of the night
When darkness hides the trees and hill
I sense his presence all around
His breath upon me still
For he in me forever dwells
And I in him abide
And not a thing can separate
The father and the child.

Towards The Kingdom

When we look as if through God's eyes we see how often it is the poorest among us who are the richest and those considered wealthy are often crippled by poverty within.

Thank you, God, for all that we do not own, for all we have not gained, for often these perceived riches are burdens holding us back on our journey towards your kingdom.

Prodigal

Sometime between now and Easter
I will die to my old self
Rise to the challenge
Of putting on a new garment
Befitting one
Who will attend a feast.

Sometime between now and Easter
In a grace-filled moment
I will rid myself of the old skin
And be cleansed in a tide of mercy
As I turn my thoughts
Towards the eternal king

Then I will bring to him his child
And he will bless me
As prodigal as one
Who comes in from the wilds.

The Curling Leaf

In a few small hours I will inherit the dawn.
And as light makes a canvas of the sky
The first broad strokes will wash the land
Where ebonised silhouettes of firs and pines
Proclaim the works of His hands.

For these and more
I will give praise and thank the Lord
For such beauty in such store-
The wakened blackbird on the leafless branch
Shafts of light on the glistening lawn
The berried rowan and the curling leaf
And the rising reddening sun.

The Thin Divide

There are days, hours of days,
Minutes of hours
When the yearning for something
Beyond all this almost overwhelms
Then from somewhere deep within my soul
There rises up like mist
A veil that separates the otherness from this,
And although I cannot see
Beyond my side of the thin divide
I sense God's presence near
As my heart stirs to embrace
Within the realms of his peace
The essence of divinity and grace.

A Lamp to Our Feet

To be blessed with a gift of faith is to be twice-blessed for faith is accompanied by long-sightedness, enabling the believer to look beyond the here and now to the promise of a life hereafter and an eternal peace. A friend of mine, a lapsed Catholic, holds the opinion that our faith is something made up to make us feel better, a sort of a crutch she says. She has not yet encountered the Cross, nor taken up its challenge - and challenge it is, day after day.

It is true of course to say our faith brings comfort and consolation in the form of the Eucharist and sacred scripture, the lives of the Saints etc.; and also in the form of encounter with other believers and non-believers whose impact on our lives can have hugely beneficial effects, and often prove to be sources of great encouragement. But often life's challenges out-number the consolations or so it would seem.

It is precisely at such times that faith comes into its own. We are blessed indeed who can draw on the vision we hold in our hearts of a kingdom prepared for us and a race to be run. And it is this belief that provides a lamp to our feet and a light for the road.

A Private Thing

Prayer is often a private thing, but when the intimate words of a soul talking to God are shared or overheard, there is often a quite striking realisation that our love of God is so powerful, that as it draws each of us closer to Him it naturally binds us together as children of one family, when we recognise in the prayers of others, the often plaintive echoes of our own heart's cry.

Creator God

When not to think of Him
Creates a loneliness within,
When not to marvel
At His work
Is narrowness of mind,
When not to listen to His word
Is poverty imposed,
Then sing, sing, sing,
Bright bird,
Red rose!

Lourdes Acrostic Poems

Light that never goes out
Our Lady of the grotto
Unsurpassed in grace and beauty
Radiant and pure
Dear Mother of God
Enable us to follow your ways
Safe in your keeping.

Lovely Lady of Lourdes
Our refuge and our hope
Universal Mother of all
Restore grace to the sinner
Dispense healing to the suffering
Enrich our hearts with love and
Secure salvation for our souls.

Grandmother

Petite, dressed in blue or black,
And, except in bed,
A crocheted hat to keep
Her pinned-up hair intact.
She always sat on the edge of a seat
As if to meet the floor half-way
With tiny, dangling feet.
Constantly at her side, a stack of little
Cards, edged black, and prayer books
Softened and dog-eared with years-
St. Anthony's Treasury,
An Hour Before the Blessed Sacrament,
Prayers to the Sacred Heart.
With glasses on the end of her nose,
She would pray for the happy repose
Of souls of relatives and friends -
Prayers of the faithful.

Light for the Road

When reflecting on aspects of my life in which there is need of healing I choose to contemplate the cross. No-one can heal better than He who healed all. No-one can conquer darkness like He who conquered death, and won for us the reward of eternal life. And so in contemplating the cross I too am raised up, that I may be healed. In contemplating the cross I contemplate salvation. And by keeping the image of the cross, like a burning flame, before me always, I am not afraid. For it is God Himself who goes before me, providing light for the road and food for the journey.

Holy Soul

Holed-up in a fortressed house
A victim of the vicissitudes of life,
He wore a tall but battered-down hat
And lived in a tweed coat too small,
Knotted cord catching the eye
Where it filled the gap
Between button-less parallels
Which seemed never destined to meet -
Much the same as he and I
Who only ever exchanged shy smiles.

Long since dead now,
Yet his figure has dogged me
On sleepless nights.
In my prayers I mention the man
With the cord round his middle,
No name, no genealogy,
Just a memory that binds,
Two stones on a foreshore
That waters made collide.

Innocence

The morning's warm air softened things,
Took the raw edge off yesterday's wound.
And the unforgettable look on a child's face
Framed in a landscape window
Gazing upward at a pair of flying swans
Spoke so eloquently of innocence, though
I could hear in a passage of echoes
My mother's cautionary voice say,
'It's rude to stare', the young child's
Wonderment was enough to hold me there.

Across The Winter Chill

Let me no more resist the tug of love
The powerful force that pulls
And raises waters to tumultuous height
And drags dense clouds across the starry night.

Let me no more resist the bidding voice
That in a whisper can unleash a war
In battlefields invisible but scarred
Where good has routed evil from its ground
Yet left me all the while unharmed

That I might speak of endless love
Of a sweet voice beckoning still
Like bird call to bird call
Across the winter chill.

Bog Wood

A tangle of brambles hung round her crafted
shoulders
Like unkempt hair fingers of wind ran through
Fingers that plucked at mildewed strings but got
no note

For all the offspring of these fertile hills knew
That even on All Souls Night
There was nothing in the world or out of it
That could raise the ghost of a sound
From a perished harp.

Thank You God for the Knowing

There is no darkness
Your light cannot penetrate
No gloom your love cannot dissipate
No burden your helping hand
Cannot alleviate
And no sin
That cannot be forgiven.

Thank you God for the knowing
You are with us until the end of time
Through the sacrifice of Calvary
We have been redeemed
Through your sacraments
We are sanctified and
By dying
We are born to life eternal.

Thy Will Be Done

Not when the weather fails us
Not when the light grows dim
But when we turn our thoughts from God
And do not let Him in,
That's when weakness gains a hold
And a little voice within
Convinces us that someone else
Will win the fight for Him.

Prayer Poem for Peace

May the light of the dawn
On that first Christmas morn
Stir hope in the hearts of men

May the peace of Christ's birth
Restore to the earth
The will to bring war to an end.

A Child of the Universe

I am a bird upon a branch of God's great tree,
I want to sing with all the strength I have in me.
I want to flit from roof to roof or paint the sky
With colours bright as morning as I fly.
I want to travel far, to see new lands
And dry my wings above the desert sands.
Or hover over woods and feel the breeze
As winds weave in and out between the trees.
But more and more the earth seems bound with chains,
As heavier and darker fall the rains,
Fewer are the places for the free
To live in peace or nest in safety.

Belfast Sunset

The sun is slipping down behind Black
Mountain
St. Peter's spires are lost to me till dawn
But in my head the pictures make a fountain
Of watercolours in tall, cascading form.
My mind reflects on suns in other cities,
A circumstance that finds us near or far,
Belfast or Beijing, our hearts are governed
By the who-ness of the persons that we are,
The knowledge of a light beyond the star.

Unto Us a Child Is Born

Will you carry him home with you, this baby who is the Christ child born of Mary on a starry night?

Do you have room for him, will you share your heart with this little infant, and let him nestle there, for in sheltering him from the ravages and rages of the world it is you who will be protected, it is you who will grow to cherish his closeness. Such intimacy is not for the faint-hearted but the courageous, not for the proud but the humble, and not for the worldly but those who set their hearts and minds on an infant treasure - a little one born of the Virgin Mary, a Prince of Peace sent into the world in the silence of a Bethlehem night, the son of God most high, a child of blessed light.

Until I Rest In Thee

Temper the wind, Lord,
Soften the ground where I lie
Let me sleep and dream
My head
Against your breast
Let me hear in the silence
Of the night the rhythmical beat
Of your heart
As I place my life
My body, my cares
In your keeping
Pray let me rest
Until the first piercing of light
Sends a rush of blood round
My cold bones
And stirs me enough
To know I have survived.

Advent

Come with me
To where we can see
The cave hewn out of rock
Where silence prevails
And darkness is all-absorbing.
From here we are bidden
To journey inward
Where peace nestles
Against ruggedness
And promises
In the unfolding of its wings
A gift of wonder
Bathed in radiant light.

Sacred Silence

Sometimes just being there is enough
When words would be an encumbrance upon
sacred silence
That lends itself so well to contemplation.

Sometimes just being there is enough
Presenting oneself, body, mind and spirit
In a act of trust
When Love pours itself out of a ruby-rimmed
cup
And all of me fills with longing.

St. Francis Xavier

It was due to an unexpected turn of events that I became familiar with the name of Francis Xavier. A vacancy arose for a caretaker at Xavier House, headquarters of the Apostolic Work in Belfast, close to our family home. This was a God-send indeed as my father had reached retirement age yet still longed to do something practical and worthwhile. He didn't hesitate, took the job and soon discovered an attractive bonus - a wilderness of walled back garden crying out for loving care. Immediately he set about weeding and feeding, planting and pruning, taking great pride in this little corner of heaven in the midst of the city. Indoors in the old airy house there was a room known as the 'Cutting Room.' A lasting memory of mine is the glorious sight of bolt upon bolt of richly coloured woven fabrics straight from the loom and from which vestments were made for every occasion in the liturgical year. Altar linens were also cut and sewn before being shipped to the missions.

St Francis Xavier responded to God's call and launched out into the deep in order to spread the Good News, and speak of the love of God, converting many souls to Christianity wherever he went. And here in this house in the north of the city was evidence that men and women centuries later were still responding to God's call.

"All power in heaven and on earth has been given to me. Go, therefore, and make disciples of all nations, baptizing them in the name of the Father, and of the Son, and of the Holy Spirit..."

Matthew 28:17-20

Offering

I offer you myself, Lord,
My sun's rising and my moon's setting,
My rain clouds and my golden rays,
I offer you my sowing and my reaping
My nights and all my days.
I offer you my dirges and my hallelujahs
My dancing and my staying still,
And by these humble offerings, Lord,
I pray to do your will
To walk along the narrow path
Where others too have trod,
The soil of earth bears but a trace
Of those who dwell with God.

I Welcome into My Heart This Night

I welcome into my heart this night
Heaven's gift
O beautiful child of light and
Prince of Peace
His presence marked by
Silence beyond words
No heaviness at all
Only quietness
Of the Christ child
Living
The Divine comforter
Loving
Healing
Holding me
In a tender embrace.

Mother Mary, Mother Mine

Mother of the Son of God
Mother of the Eternal Word
Mother of the child divine
Mother Mary, Mother mine.

Mother of Immanuel
Mother of the child of light
Mother of the sun and stars
Mother of the day and night.

Mother chaste and Mother pure
Mother meek and Mother mild
Listen to my prayer and pleading
As a mother heeds her child.

Listen to a world that's weeping
Bring to Jesus all our sighs
Change hard hearts to glad hearts beating
As our many voices rise.

We who are your earthly children
Look to you in heaven above
Ask of you a Mother's blessing
Find in you a Mothers love.

Easter Poem

Fruits in faraway orchards are gleaming
Flower-heads from snow-covered valleys peep
All now on earth and in heaven is singing
Knowing Our Lord is no longer asleep.

Birds on high wires
And sweet-sounding waters
Steeples in mist
And clouds rolling high
Are in one voice and one motion united
Praising the Lord of the earth and the sky.

O triumph of Easter
O rapturous reigning
The darkness of death for all time overcome
We worship, bow down and forever adore you,
The Father, the Son, the Spirit in one.

Redeemer and Victor
High Priest and Saviour
Innocent Lamb who on Calvary died
Great is the mystery
Powerful the message
He who was dead
Is raised up
Is Alive!

Is Alive!

Patrick on Slemish Mountain

I gazed up at the sky and saw a field:
Stars scattered like seed on darkest soil,
And where the moon advanced no cloud
concealed
A watchful eye above a world of toil,
While later, through the thinning dark converged
Ascending notes of dawn-addressing birds.

Belfast Morning Walk

I wakened to the sound of bird-song and was made keenly aware of the chill of the March morning as I inhaled the outside air. I thanked God for my heart and my soul, for the highs and the lows, the days of light and shade. I thanked him for the nearby hills, and all the works of his hands - right down to the feather lodged among the bulrushes by the pond's edge and in the stately form of a stranger by the church steps.

It was a blessed and peaceful day, a gift from one who alone can make the deaf hear and the blind see. For it is he who is in the rainbow above the school-yard, in the red flash of a robin in a holly tree as the cortège winds its way to a last resting place, in the spontaneity of the child splashing in the mirror shallows of a puddle, in the clump of pink heather in the rockery, and in the gap-toothed smile of an old woman bravely but surely plodding her way home.

Precious Years

The grasses sway and all of a sudden
They are under the spell of the wind
As the child tosses the leaf from her hand
And watches it swirl and twirl its way
Sucked under the bridge's darkness
Emerging smaller now
Almost lost in a race of water
That reflects the sky's steely grey.

Suddenly his head knows what his heart has
locked away:
A day will come
When there will be another letting go
Another twirling
And swirling into the world
Like a flake in a flurry of snow.

Maybe he will return here then
And peer into the water to watch the passage
Of clouds like great puffed-up carriages
Wheeling through a Disney tale,
But this is all there is for now
And it is sweetly real.

Children of God

I've spoken with individuals who consider themselves estranged from the church. Sometimes their situation has come about as the result of hurt suffered at a sensitive time in their lives, or a brush with someone seen as representative of the church, or more often than not a case of disillusionment or a sense of not fitting in.

It's hard to convince such a person that it is infinitely better to be part of the church with all its imperfections than to cut oneself off from it. How can we expect to get something out if we put nothing in; what good are our talents if we keep them to ourselves, hoarded away like money in a cash tin? A church community thrives when those within it pool together for the greater good.

Everyone has something to offer God, and something to share for God's sake. By coming together to worship Him, we can stumble upon hidden gifts and at the same time become healed of the hurt and division which otherwise would keep us apart.

There will be no fanfare for an estranged soul coming back into the fold (at least none we can hear) nor will it be roses all the way, but there is for them what there is for us, namely, real communion and the confirming of our identity as children of God.

Church

In the chapel especially it comes to me - an awareness of the hunger of the soul - hunger that nothing in this world can satisfy. I and others are drawn into this sacred space as towards the warmth and light of a fire, bringing with us our cares and concerns, our hopes and fears. We come to God's house in our brokenness, aware that there is healing there at all times, and in the stillness and in the quiet, somehow the going in and the coming out are never the same.

Ardglass Harbour

One old fishing boat rests
Against a tide-marked wall,
Its timbers skinned
Warped and water-whitened,
The wheel-house gutted.
Suddenly, alarming cries pierce the air
As the 'Silver Harvester' comes in,
Bulging nets of herring are
Lowered into crates,
Ice like milky quartz is shovelled on top.
Glazed dead eyes
Reflect the bird-whitened sky.
In the harbour now two seals,
Then one, then nothing but bubbles
Bursting on bright water.

Mary, Mother of God

How blessed are we
Who call you, Mary,
Who call you, Mother.

How can it be?
That we are yours,
You, who are the Mother of God.

You plead for us,
And in your love
You pray for us sinners
In our unworthiness-
How can it be?

How blessed are we
Who know your love
And that of your beloved Son.

How blessed are we,
Who call you, Mary,
Who call you, Mother,
O Holy Immaculate One.

Grace and Light

We are beneficiaries of light
Receivers of Our Lady's grace
That irrigates the arid plains
Of hearts adrift and wills untamed
And makes of soul a sacred place
Undefiled and peace-contained
Where Son of God can enter in
Rest upon its furnishings
And there protect and best defend
The temple walls from raids of men
For none can breach what none can rend
As grace and light transform, transcend.

Mary's Watch

Mary is in night's quiet
When the valleys are folded in sleep
And a layering of mist
Muffles the urban dark.

She is in day's light
When veils are raised
And revelations are
Like market-stalls arrayed.

She is in the sorrow
That rakes the memories
Of heart and mind
Grieving for what is gone.

She is in joy
In perpetual outpourings of love
That holds us in the womb of time
Secure and unafraid.

She is with God
Holy in the grace of knowing

Hers is a voice, a call
Heard more as longing in the soul

Finding answer in the dawn of prayer.

Mending Nets

For Sean Savage

We mend our nets
By attending to the gaps
In our defences.

If we are to bring something back
Something to show for our day's work
How foolish to run the risk of losing it

We have only one life
We mend our nets
And we keep going.

198

The Little Ones

For my friends at Edmund Rice PS Belfast

From ancient four year olds
I've witnessed little acts of forgiveness

An arm flung round another's shoulder
A lantern smile flashed across a room

Such little ones have little to learn
Innocence wears its graces

The spark of love in children's eyes
The God-child in their faces.

Assumption of the Blessed Virgin Mary

No earthly tomb
For a body ever-blessed
Assumed into heaven
Angel-borne to the golden throne
Of her beloved Son reigning in eternal glory
With the Father and the Spirit
Holy, holy, holy.

No earthly tomb for the
Chosen God-bearer
Virgin most pure
Heavenly honour is hers
Beyond what can corrupt or stain
Prevail against, deface or mar
The jewel set in Mary's crown:
Dawn's grace and evening's star.

His Holy Name

In this secular world
There is one belief I hold dear:
I am a child of God,
I belong to Him who is perfect love.
He is my most valued friend,
My loving and constant protector.
May I never lose sight of His face,
Never cease to speak His holy name
For fear He should become
One of the 'Disappeared',
Taken and ruthlessly silenced
Year after long-suffering year.

Holy Temple

A visitor came calling at my door
Inviting me to pray
I was busy with my chores
He went away.

A visitor came calling
Hoping to stay
In the quiet night
I muttered some excuse
He took flight.

A visitor came calling at my door
Voice soft as a breeze
My heart ached sore
I put him at ease.

The house is yours, I said,
He entered in
In lighted candle glow
I welcomed him.

*"My thoughts are not your thoughts,
my ways, not your ways – it is the Lord who
speaks. Yes, the heavens are as high above earth
as my ways are above your ways, my thoughts
above your thoughts." Isaiah 55:8-9*

The Birthday of the Blessed Virgin Mary

Blessed are you, sweet Mother
And blessed are Joachim and Anne
And all in your childhood years
Who were parts of God's rich plan.

Blessed the Annunciation
Blessed the Virgin birth
And blessed too are we,
Your family here on earth.

As we come before you
To mark this special day
We bring to you sweet roses
And blooms that breezes sway

Their perfume rises upward
As incense on the air
As tribute to your Queenship
As emblem of your care.

The Breath of God

The world is alive
With the breath of God
Inhaling and exhaling
We are blessed
With a sense of newness
Of awareness
Of renewal

Immersing our old selves in fresh
Springs of grace
Cleansing our dusty souls
In the waters of salvation

We rejoice in
The new day's light
In the Godly affirmation
That we are in the palm of his hand
That God is with us
That we are never alone.

Memories

For Charles McCormick

He spoke of an unforgettable
Journey to the Holy Land
Of being on a boat
On a beautiful day
On the Sea of Galilee
A sea of starry light
When a powerful feeling seized him
As a calming faith assured him
That he, too, with eyes fixed on his Master
Could walk on water.

One Day in Your House

Often the most meaningful dialogue is not that which takes place round a conference table or in a committee room; but that which takes place between God and us in the confines of our hearts. Within the walls of His house there is a dispensary of divine proportion where mercy and grace and love are poured out. The gentle voice that has echoed down centuries still resounds today within these walls ready to engage in dialogue private and profound. We may come before Him downcast or bewildered, heavily burdened or holding nothing back, but we come as one into the Father's house. He smiles on us in our coming and blesses us in our going. His house is our family's – God's family's - gathering place, a home until we reach our final home, a place of shelter from life's storms and gales, a source of joy and endless love.

"One day in your house is worth a thousand elsewhere."

Psalm 84

Do Not Keep Them from the Door

For Sr Eleanor OCSO

Do not keep them from the door
Usher them in
Open the windows
Let them circulate round every room
And floor
Let them waft and weave
Their wares, their fragrances -
Do not keep them from the door:
The airs and graces of the morning
The maids and mysteries
Of a new day dawning.

Counting

For Bronagh

I watch her skip
If I were able to halt
The rope at the moment
When it arches above her head
I would wish that she
Might be protected
From all harm, safe within
The space her arms create.
She urges me to watch, to help her count.
So, by listening
To her small feet hit the ground
With a lightness of touch
I count,
For one who counts so much.

In Memory Of My Father

I think of him now as one
Who breathes the eternal Word,
Whose veins are awash
With April rains,
Whose eyes reflect God's beauty
And a light that time cannot outshine
Or dim
For him all is ordered now and right.
He is not old or weak or slow now

And this one thing I know:
His faith was strong,
It was his anchorage in life,
He knew when to hold on,
When to let go,
And left to Providence
All he did not know.

Enduring Love

My Love will not smother you.
Think of it rather
Like the darkness that descends
And enfolds the flower in bud
But then at the daylight hour
There bursts forth from night's grip
A beautiful blue rose.
You, too, are free
To grow, to choose, to bloom,
But remember this:
My Love endures,
Remains unchanged,
You are mine always
Receive
Believe.

The Journeyman

It took darkness
For me to grope for light
It took a starless night
For me to see the moon
It took aridity
For me to thirst for God
It took hunger
For me to search for food.
It took abandonment
For me to meet a friend
It took selfishness
To get to that dead-end
It took blindness
For me to finally see
The God of Life
The God of Love
The God in me.

Precious Pearls

Today it is heavy, Lord,
This heart of mine.
Like a berried rowan after snow
It weeps in the shadows
When no one is near enough to hear
And sighs like the wind
Weaving its way through the towering trees -
Can you hear it, Lord?
Can you hear it heave?
What am I asking?
For is it not The Spirit
That breathes on me?
And is it not the Father
Who counts the days and
Weighs all things?
To You, then I will fly, I will cling,
For in the closing of my eyes, You are near,
And I can hear on mystic trails
Truths flow like treasure from a chest:
Strung pearls spilling out across the darkness.

Fields of Praise

Beauty is but a leap away
For those who step out under the stars
Sown across the sky
Like countless seed in
Midnight fields of praise.

Beauty is but a reach away
For those who climb the stairway
Of the skies and let fall a tread so light
As makes no dent
On the wide and moon-trailed compress
Of the night.

Who? Tell Me, Who?

What Love
Could endure such suffering
Surely no blameless One ever existed-
A man like us in all things but sin?
Who would do this?
Lay down his life for others-
Unknown souls
Generations apart,
Who would do this
In obedience to a Father?
Who would die on a cross?
Who? Who? Tell me Who?
Who but Jesus, Prince of Peace,
Redeemer and Saviour
He did
And He does
He is
As He was
But Risen now, death-defying
Crowned in glory
Coming in glory,
With the Father and the Spirit,
Holy, Holy, Holy.
I adore You, my Jesus
I adore You, my Lord
I adore You, my King.

In Him

I have said yes
I am not afraid
For who would shrink back from light
After having walked in darkness?
Who would spurn bread and water
After a night in the desert?
Who would turn their eyes
From the Book of Wisdom,
Or their back on Love
When the longing of
Heart and soul
Are met here, now,
In Him?
I have said yes.
My heart is at peace.
I am not afraid.

Beauty of God

Perhaps when you hear the bell ring out across the valley you will think about what it is to pray. Where will you find beauty this day? Maybe you will see it in the face of a friend, or in the bright eyes of a child, or a fragrance or hue will remind you of summer flowers in lush meadows. You may be humbled by the beauty of the artwork on a prison cell wall, or in the lean and lined face of an octogenarian whose once labour-coarsened hands are now soft as a baby's.

Maybe you will hear beauty speak to your soul through strains of music or the sounds of the sea; or you will encounter it in the very depths of suffering when visiting someone you know whose life is wound round the wood of the Cross. The truth is beauty is never far away; it surrounds us and is within. Thus we who are made in the image and likeness of the loving God have much to celebrate amidst our pain, and much to sing about amidst our suffering. God and beauty are inseparable. God is in the beautiful, and we are in God. We trust and place our hope in Him who supports and sustains us.

Mother Mary

Flower of Heaven
Flower so rare
Each petal a pattern of holiness.
Regal raiment of star-bright whorls
Dipped in purest light
Crowned with diamonds
Diamonds bright
Mother of all
Mother of Christ.

The Holy Bible

In between the leaves
In between the lines
In between the words
Are the little spaces
Where one can
Inhale the fragrance
That exudes from
This repository of grace
This fount of wisdom.

And as I do so I am carried in mind
As you once carried this book
To God's place
His house of
Holy oils and lace
And linen and marble
And water and wood
Carved and lathed;
Stained glass
And brass and iron
And incense and flame,
And presence,
Yes, presence:
Real and proclaimed.

The Seafarer

You'd find him by the water's edge at dusk
Perched like a tern on granite
Or picking his way among rock pools
His hands in his pockets.
And on a peaceful night
He could be heard singing a slow air
The notes ascending the briny darkness;
And although there was a lonesomeness
About him
He seemed content by the sea
Sensing in its ebbing and flowing
The greatest of mystery
Enchanted by mesmeric power
That at once was rhythmic and slack
The horizon forever before him
The voluminous dunes at his back.

The rivers have raised their voices

Psalm 92

The rivers have raised their voices
They clap their hands and sing
Of the glorious, victorious
Christ, Our Lord and King.
Conqueror of death
Saviour of mankind
Risen Lord and Master
Bathed in a light Divine.
Mountains and deserts and oceans
Sing of His wondrous praise
And forests and valleys are ringing
As rivers their choruses raise.

The God who through all godliness prevails

The God who through all godliness prevails
Soars like a seabird above waves
Waves that have thundered height on height
Height that has breached the walls of night
Night that concedes to flowers of light
Light lived in faith that never fails
In the God who through all godliness prevails.

Autumn Poem

For Ann D'Arcy

Even when the last leaf
Is past its clinging on
And tree after tree in the forest
Sings a soulful, leafless song
The seedlings of the fruits of spring
Are dreams that are coming on
In the mulch of imagination
Round the mists of a watery dawn.

The Presentation of the Blessed Virgin Mary

How they loved
This longed-for child
How their eyes danced
At the first glance of God's beautiful gift.

One happy year, then two, then before
They knew it they were moved
To bring Mary to the Temple.

Ascending the steps the little one smiled,
Wisdom before, Wisdom behind,
And as they watched with misted eyes
A voice said "Hope! Be reconciled!

I go into this holy place
Where all is light and all is grace,
The gift of life you've given me
Will bear the fruit to set men free.

I dedicate myself to God -
These temple walls do not divide
The love of those contained herein
From that which flows outside.

I shall take you in my heart
To where I do not know
As we are wont to follow where
The Spirit bids us go.

So not in sadness do you leave
Nor I in sadness stay
For we are in the Spirit's love
Day unto gifted day."

Folds Above

The Holy Spirit spreads its wings
And all the choirs of heaven sing
As a bride of Christ comes home.
A leaf is loosed from yonder tree
To spiral downward on the breeze
But what to human eyes seems lost
Is raised, renewed, as change is wrought
And that which to the branch did cling
Now sails on high like angel wings
And she to whom God looks in love
Is nestled now in folds above.

A Place to Belong

When you have gathered about you
A rich tableau of fields,
When listeners with felt-lidded eyes
Are asleep in burrows and hedgerows,
Hold on to the ledge
Where you dream your best dreams
And lean out into the night
Turn your face toward
The sky
Towards the clay
And imagine
The invisible forms high and low
That only a few hours before
Wore the colours of day-
Then pay heed to the urge within you
Give voice to the song
That finds in the darkness
A place to belong.

Leaves

God is here they said
Shy whisperings of praise
Arms raised in
Graceful movements

Open to heaven's gaze.
God is near they said
And I looked and looked at the leaves
And imagined the roots,
Sap rising, feeding,
Giving each leaf its form,
Its identity, its life.

God is here they said
And in their wild colours I saw
The palette of His hand
And in their number
A multiplicity
Like stars,
Or grains of sand.

Our Lady of Sorrows

Mary's pain defies words.
Lone notes rise
Stark as bird-cries
Across February snows

Tears flow like amber beads on bark
Grievous the seven wounds
That penetrate her heart.

Prayer

For Sr Grace

There is a tree that draws its food from silence
Whose upturned leaves are raised like hands in
prayer
Whose blossoms pour forth a powerful fragrance
That wafts like incense borne upon the air.

There is a flower that blooms amid the desert
In arid lands that hear no sweet refrain
But then from high above fall heaven's riches
That feed and nurture through the falling rains.

Transformation

A forty day call to holiness
Through prayer to the Father
Through fasting in desert loneliness
And journeying far beyond the familiar
Until we reach that place,
An oasis, a garden of fruit
Round which pitched tent roofs are
Pierced by perfect truths
And the giver of life
Is revealed in shimmering stars.

Gethsemane

Even those who love me sleep.
The night is long and
Through these red hours of agony
My body trembles
And my heart is heavy at the thought
Of what the day will bring.
But Father, I am here to do your will,
And though my mouth is dry with fear
And although I cry and cry,
It is thy cup I now take up,
I will not pass it by.

Good Friday

An impassioned mist enveloped those
Who stood beneath the Cross
No ordinary man was this -
A veil of mourning covered the sun,
The temple curtain was torn from top to base,
The cold earth quaked as
All were plunged into an ecliptic night
When even the wood of Calvary stood
Bereft of heaven's light.

Within The Wounds

Somewhere within the wounds
There is a language deeper than words
Deeper than wells
Deeper than woods

Somewhere within the wounds
There is the fragrance
Of love, of gift,
A heart of sacredness
An altar of the lamb
Somewhere within the wounds
Is where Christ is
And where I,
In my unworthiness,
Am.
Somewhere within the wounds
Petals unfurl
As the flower of His sacred passion
Is loosed onto the world.

Good Shepherd

We come to you, Lord,
As lambs bound
At the sound of the shepherd's
First foot-fall.
And in coming before you we pray
For your protection
And your blessings each day,
And we pray too
For those who are lost or scattered far.
We are hopeful that with time and grace
All be gathered into one fold
With you as the Good Shepherd
And us in our true home.

The Voice That Calls

Attend to the voice that calls
Wafting in
Above warm sills
Down airy halls
Through leafy gaps
Through webbed crevices in sunlit walls
Attend to the voice that calls.
From the unfathomable deep
From stonecrop peaks
Riding on waves of sound
Moving on currents of air
Attend, attend if you dare
Attend to the voice that calls.

Sacred Heart Poem

None such as us
Is outside his love
None falls so far
Into the abyss
To be beyond his reach

With heart open
And mercy all-encompassing
He inclines towards us in readiness
Responding to the faintest

Hint of light
The least crack
In the cold stone wall of denial
And then
With power indisputable
He transforms
Bit by bit
Rendering grace upon grace
Changing the wastelands of men's souls
Into pastures fit for paradise.

Lourdes 2009

Gazing at one tiny violet
Centres the mind
For at its heart
There is nothing but the radiating gold
Of life's promise
One flower is enough
To bring down from heaven
The rain of the future
The light of tomorrow
To produce
More violets
More flowers
For the crown of glory.

Corpus Christi Prayer

Corpus Christi, nourish me
For your body is food indeed,
The Bread of life.
Corpus Christi, flood my soul
Cleanse me of all sin,
In streams of mercy and love
Engulf me.
Corpus Christi,
Direct my steps
For Your way leads to truth -
There is no other.
Corpus Christi, live in me,
Animate me
That I might live always in You.

God's Gold

Nothing that I have is mine
Nothing that I hold
For all is dust and all is nought
But that which is God's gold;
The witness of our lives here now
The measure still to come
The majesty and ecstasy
When the race is run
Is all that should engage my heart
In all, for all and through
The darkness into endless light
From blackness into blue
Of skies that draw the eyes and mind
Above the world's dull din
And elevate and irrigate
The arid land within.

Dusk

For as long as I can remember
I have had an affinity with dusk

Of quiescence
When day loses its thrust
And night puts on display
Its first dim show
Of seed pearls shimmering in watery light

But all is changed when darkness gains a hold
And marigolds
With fiery eyes ignite the sky and make of high
and low
A secret garden
In which to air one's dusky soul.

Our Lady of the Wayside

Pray for your children
Wherever they may be
Let your motherly hand guide us
Along the winding paths of life
And lead us joyfully
To life eternal

The Bosom of Abraham

The 'bosom of Abraham' is one of those phrases that seem to be reserved mostly for funeral rites. These words are in the Prayer of Commendation towards the end of the funeral mass. For those not familiar with it, here it is:

May Christ, who called you, take you to himself; may angels lead you to the bosom of Abraham.

To which the response is:
Receive his (her) soul and present him (her) to God the Most High.

At the time of bidding farewell, amid great sadness, when the body is incensed and blessed for the last time, the use of these hope-filled words bestows such loving dignity on the soul - all the more poignantly so in the case of one who may have had little dignity afforded them in life.

Death is never the victor. It may strip the body of its faculties, the mind of its reason, the heart of its vitality, but the soul it cannot touch. We are God's through and through and in dying life is changed, not ended.

If Mary Were Garment

If Mary were garment
She would be white as
Woven strands of light
Topped with crowns of edelweiss.
If she were jewel
She would be diamond-bright.
If she were flower
The sun on her would gaze
Mesmerized by beauty
But Mary is more than this;
Mary is heaven's Queen
Immaculate and pure
Grace-filled and serene
Mary is intercessor
And from heaven above
She nurtures
And protects us
And raises us
To Love.

Mary Immaculate

Mary Immaculate
Model heart of love
And motherhood
Look to your children
With eyes of mercy.

Wrap us in garments
Of unfolding grace
Protect us against all evil and harm
And help us persevere
In faith.

Stay close to us, Most Holy Queen
So that we remain
United with you
Blessed in the life of the Trinity.

Still Small Voice

The presence of God is like a lamp that is always lit, its flame inextinguishable. When the lights are off and the doors safely locked and bolted, the sanctuary lamp in the church burns on to signify the real abiding presence of God in the tabernacle, just as in the darkest gloomiest moments of our lives God is present as that still small voice, ever-ready to listen, ever-loving, ever-near. In our joys and in our sorrows, in our laughter and in our tears the constancy of the love of God is a beacon of hope - a light that will never go out.

The Heron

Right by the water's edge
It bears an understated gracefulness with
Twig-thin legs ably balancing
Its body weight.
Yellow eyes are sharp
As its razor beak.
The turn of the neck
So sinuous so defined

I wish I could will it into flight
To witness the black breadth
Of its wing span
The prowess of take-off
Its silent might.

Our Lady of the Rosary

Our Lady of the Rosary,
Pray for us
That in these prayerful mysteries
We may draw closer to the truth.
In their joyfulness
May we be more joyful.
In their sorrowfulness
May we enter into Christ's passion
As we accept the trials of life.
And in their gloriousness
May we never lose hope
That we too will one day be raised up
To share the joy of heaven
In our eternal home.

Way of Truth

Immaculate Heart of Mary, educate me in the
way of truth.
Let me cling to faith as a child clings to its
mother's garment,
Let me never be too afraid or ashamed to come
to you,
To confide in you,
No matter how far I may wander from grace,
Let me know always that you,
In your maternal tenderness
Will always care for me;
And with eyes of mercy and
Gestures of forgiveness
You will welcome me into the folds
Of your goodness, the mantle of your charity
The heart of your motherly love.

The Rosary

For Celine and Ailish

I remember the image of the beads'
Reflection on the pale chapel wall
How, when the sun poured in and
Projected their prismatic colours
They danced like fairy-lights
As they shimmered and swayed in a loop

And how, if I watched for long enough,
The crucifix would turn full circle
Worked through her fingers
The mysteries complete.
I knew well the countdown to home-time:
The kissing of the Lord's feet,
The bedding of the beads
Eased like liquid crystal
Into a creased purse,
The Sign of the Cross and
Head-bowed genuflection.

Sanctifying the Moment

I cannot separate
My world from God's.
In all things
Sweet or bitter
He is near.
In those whom I encounter
In any situation
I need only pause
Long enough
To gather
The threads of knowledge
The strands that together
Weave a fabric
Of His being
That transforms my coming and going
My time of work
And time of rest into
A giving and receiving
A living and loving
In Him.

A Silent Corner

In real and abiding awe
I come before your presence.
To that which eye cannot see
Or ear hear
I lend my senses
Secure in the belief
That you, O Lord,
Do see, and do hear me.

Time seems far removed
And the world a distant place
Yet if I step outside this space
Or turn my thoughts towards
Worldly things
I realise at once that
This is no real place apart.

A silent corner in a busy world
Encapsulates for me
Time enough to balance thoughts
Room enough to breathe
The incensed air of sacredness
That brings me to my knees.

The Visitation

Kinship and kindness meet
Bringing Mary far,
Road-weary
And excited at the thought of
Greeting Elizabeth.

And did that child leap!
What joy to behold
What joy foretold
Babes not yet born
Enjoined in love
In mysterious bliss
And mother-cousins
Heaven-blessed and radiant
With life.

Prayer for the Day

I will be tolerant this day
Judging no-one I meet
Bearing patiently what comes my way
I will not grumble or complain
I will not mock
Or covet
What someone else has got.

Today I will bring Jesus into the world
And show His loving face
To the oppressed and lonely
Or those burdened by disgrace.
Today I will give something away
And yet will feel no loss
For Jesus gave his all for all
To death upon a cross.

I will be tolerant this day
And at its peaceful close
I will take time to think about
Past hours as each unfolds
Time to ask forgiveness
Time to bless and praise
Time to trust to God alone
The world and all its ways.

The Lord hears the cry of the poor

The Lord hears the cry of the poor and a response comes from within our own hearts.

God-in-us is what motivates us to do what we can to alleviate poverty and injustice. When we give alms, fund-raise or fast we are engaging in acts of solidarity with those who are poor. We can encourage each other and be proud of our efforts but we can never be complacent – not while there is hunger and inequality in the world. All that is good in us, all that is love, comes from God, and in serving Him we serve our brothers and sisters. So much money is squandered or accumulated, so much food wasted while many millions of people go without. The choices we have are extensive – which cereal to eat at breakfast, which mode of transport to use, where to go on vacation etc. Yet for many there are no such choices. A hungry mother in Ethiopia might well raise her eyes to heaven, asking where God is, and the answer may come in the next convoy of humanitarian aid or the care she receives at a mission clinic or hospital. And here at home there are many poor living among us. It was reported last Christmas that some people who had in previous years made donations to the St Vincent De Paul Society found themselves having to ask for help instead such is the effect of the credit crunch on unemployment figures.

God is a generous giver and we are his appointed stewards; we are the carers and sharers of all creation. The mandate we have been given, no matter what our vocation, is to love. We cannot separate ourselves from the poor because we and they are one in Christ. When the poor cry to God, love wills us into action. And action is proof of his love.

"This poor man cried, and the Lord heard him: and saved him out of all his troubles."

Psalm 34:6

Wake House

We stand patiently
Hoping that what we are about to say
Will bring comfort or
Momentarily stem the
Tears streaming
From raw-rimmed eyes

Later
At a time that will hardly register
Amidst the great flurry of things happening
And not happening
The family will have the freedom
To be themselves for a while
As they set about
Turning out the room –
The temple of their lives –
That death and we
Have so unceremoniously shot through.

Soul's Sweet Guest

For Patricia Wade

To rest in him
Mind and heart
Is to enter into that realm
Blessed
With the nearness of
The soul's sweet Guest.
Awareness of the divine-come-down
Present within me now
Fills me with awe.
As I commune with him
I ask myself a hundred times
Is this for real?
This gift
This liberty
Is the all-powerful almighty God
My soul's guest, the keeper of its key?
My soul answers
With the truth -
He delights in me.

Seen and Unseen

Each season claims its own
And they depart
Swift as snow upon a sunlit green
Seen then unseen,
God's works of art.
But memories are kindling
For the fire that burns
In the grate of time.
And the stoker's eye
Sees face after face arrayed
Expressions and postures
Curiously displayed.

Old men with sticks
A sheepdog at a gate
Laughing young girls with curls arranged;
Much as sculptures in a bright arcade

Yet one by one the figures fall
And to the earth return
All, all.

Two or Three…

Characteristic irregularity
Of floor-trailing feet is
My cue to watch and wait
While she side-steps
Into her favourite seat;
Then with an awkward
Movement of her head,
She turns towards me
Across the aisle
And smiles, then waves
And makes a face that says
'It's cold outside', as she
Blows make-shift heat
Into her bloodless hands.
This bond of ours
Commands few words,
The air is silent, deep.
Much is pondered in the heart
Of which the lips daren't speak.

A Little Prayer for You

I pray God will shine His light on you always,
That no darkness may ever overshadow you,
That no fear may ever hold you back,
Nor desire overwhelm, but that of loving
And serving Him all the days of your life.

A Moment Such As This

In a moment such as this
I am a vessel of God's grace
Yet suddenly and jealously
Dark clouds can hide His face
And keep from me the very source
From which God's blessings flow,
If untended and unguarded
Stands the doorway to my soul.

Mary's Song

The sweetest voice sings on
And heaven is graced
With a Marian love song.

The Blessed Virgin
Is the eternal rose of time
Of past, present and promise still to come,
Body and soul assumed
United with the beloved Bridegroom.

Here on earth motherly love surrounds
Light as a veil that falls upon the world
Where noon bells sound
From lowlands and hills
Through void and throng
In ancient halls
The calling gong
Strikes on and on

From age to age
From east to west
With Mary's grace
The world is blessed.

Peace and Light

For Paddy Gaffikin

Dear God, give me the courage to stand up and
be counted,
To say yes when those around me are saying no,
To knock on the door that others pass by.
Give me the courage to wear the badge of faith
with pride
To count myself among the fortunate and the
blessed and
To carry the light of my faith into the world.
Grant me that peace the world cannot give.
Let it reign always in my heart
That I might bear witness to
The light of your truth
The power of your divinity
And the triumph of the cross.

A Blessed Moment

Nothing has seemed the same since then
Neither hill nor stream
Nor the pine trees' morning scent.
Even the cawing of crows in the glen
Seems changed, seems different.

The light on the lake
Was a pool of grace
No cloud marred the blueness above
Blessed were we and holy the place
That mirrored God's perfect love.

The Truth Will Hold

The truth will hold
Just as good as God is good
And God is good all told.

The light will lead
Just as bright as God is bright
And God is bright all told,
All night

Truth and light
Will hold and lead
For God is truth
And God is light
And truth is light indeed.

Flora and Stone

I can look out into the deepest night
And know that in darkness
Seen and unseen take on new meaning
In the language of believers.

In visions most beautiful
God is present to me
In slender swaying grasses of the fields,
In the wood anemone
That turns its yellow eye towards the faintest
Intimation of light;
Or the yellow-billed blackbird at dusk
Bold and lustrous in its song

Even the grey stone walls and hedgerows
Hemming the fields
Defining for each his place
In this undulating landscape
Sing God's praise;
While I too am caught up in ritual
Lauding the aspects of nature
In facets of flora and stone.

Poem of Praise

To praise is to fly towards Him who made us
To liberate our spirit wings
And all that binds our minds
And nails us down
As creatures forlorn.

To praise is to raise our thoughts
To new terrain
From where we see beyond what blinds
To the beauty of the grain
Hidden under bark in darkness
Waiting for the craftsman's plane.

To praise is to fly towards Him who made us
To repose in the life within
To amplify and glorify
To raise the voice and sing.

Advent Poem

Bless my soul, Lord,
At this time of waiting
And anticipation.

May your word be as benediction
As I prepare the way for
The sovereign child
The Prince of Peace
Whose throne is clay
Whose realm is
The tabernacle of
The human heart
That bids him stay.

Bless my soul, Lord,
At this time of waiting
For the promised one.
Let my creation be
A dwelling place fit for a king -
The Son of God most high
Who comes as light, as joy,
As flame-setter within…

Then, like the shepherds of long ago
I, too, will worship him.

Irish Christmas Blessing

Let the Christ light be fastened
To the lintel above the door
Let it be as candle-glow in the window
That speaks of homeliness
Of welcome and warmth.

May the Christ child
Bring peace that finds its place
In restful solitude
As well as in throng,
In action as well as in word.

May the baby Jesus and his Blessed Mother
Be twin shields against evil and harm
And harbingers of the joy that is ours
And all that is yet to come.

I Am a Child of God

Placed in the cradle of his ageless knowing
There is a part of me
That has not yet reached its prime.
Like the bed of a river
That is composed of histories
Laid down by its flowing water
Impressed upon my soul is
A story all its own
A tale of dying to the old world
And of being born into the new
The riddling and sifting
His journeying through.

New Year Poem

Some speak of lives
Long or short-lived
But in truth
The time that is ours
That promised to us
Stretches to infinity

Let us be busy then -
Let no window refuse
The Light of Christ
May His goodness
Illuminate
Penetrate
Every pane, every corner
Until the soul of the house
Like crystal shines
In the light of the sun
And the walls of the house
Are but veils
Lifting to new horizons.

In God We Know There is Completeness

Nothing missing
No part unfulfilled
In God we see
The totality
Of goodness and grace
The essence of divinity revealed.

And yet in God
We see brokenness
The bloodied human face of
The fallen cross-bearer
The mockery that was made
Of a thorn-crowned king.

Thus we arrive at holy ground
Where the God of completeness
And the God of humanity meet
Round the altar
At the sacrifice of love.

Eternal Day

For Fr Billy Fulton

In our sorrows, Lord
We taste your suffering
And in our loneliness
That garden dark
Where all are silent,
Lost or sleeping
Save you alone, dear Lord
With aching heart.

In our joy, dear Lord
We savour wholeness.
In your rising we are raised up
When all of purity
And all of goodness
Is poured abundantly
From passion's cup.

In our living, Lord
We walk in shadow
Your presence with us
Along life's way
And in our giving, Lord
We build the kingdom
That opens up for us
Eternal day.

Patrick

To do as Patrick did is to pray
All the hours long
Making of dull labour
An incensed song.

To do as Patrick did is to be humble
To rid the soul of darkness
To hold the glass up to the light.

To do as Patrick did is to let nothing
Come between oneself and God's love.

To do as Patrick did
Is to live in the Blessed Trinity
To walk in the shadow of love
Heart and mind high-pinned on
The hope of heaven.

To do as Patrick did
Is to convert the world
Starting at the mountain path within.

Soul to Soul

We are branches that connect
One to another
Soul to soul
Like a blackbird
On a hazel bush at dawn
Wiring a song to God.

We are psalmists of his love,
Roving tabernacles
In which the prince resides
Bearing his peaceful presence
Into the busy marketplace of life.

Lent

Lent is a thread to a secret love song
Planted passionately in the soul.
We raise our eyes to the steeple
On the fir-flanked hill
As the bell tolls,
For we are a watchful people.

We prepare for times of holiness
As we process toward the triduum:
Christ's agonizing end

His descent into hell
Then all the unlocked wounded mystery
Of death-defying glory.

Earth Hour Poem

For Fr Senan Timoney SJ

Some say there is a song within the soul
Only God can hear
A melody composed on strings of joy
As lark song high and clear
Is mellifluous to the celestial ear.

Some say the soul composes while we sleep
Nocturnes that flower among the stars
Turning night air sweet
Yet stirring not the skeletons of trees
Stiff upon a sea of umber grief.

To Jesus through Mary

We are led by a guiding star
The gentlest of teachers
Perfect model of adorer
Before the adored,
As we learn humility
At the school of Mary.

All that flows
And emanates from
His Real Presence
Is a river of golden grace
Jesus offers to us
Through his mother -
We, too, are children of Mary,
Brothers and sisters in one
And Mary is as light that leads
Through her,
To her own Son.

Good Friday 2010

There are no words for that moment
When the temple veil was rent
As darkness overtook the hours
Or when water and blood streamed
To form a pool that seeped
Into the fleshy veins beneath
His wounded side.
There are no words for scenes
Like these
Yet there is a prayer
Constant in its inexpressible grief.
A cry on lips that reaches heaven
A breaking of the heart
That bruises nature
And shrouds the world.

Easter

Easter is as kindling to the soul
As infiltrating light on forest floor
As vapours from the fallow fields that rise
When sunlight penetrates the hardened core.
Easter is the flower of hope in him
That carried in our hearts seeds all we do
The risen Lord becomes alive in us
His joy is ours, and Easter ever-new.

Chapel Visitation

I come to you today laden with emptiness
No ready answers to the hows or whys
No deposits of knowledge to soothe the weeping
All too deep the wounding and the sighs.

I come in sorrow,
Though with nothing proffered
As balm for the rawness of your pain
But I pray that in the emptiness I offer
A kernel of beyondness will remain

That in its own good time will come to surface
And blossom in the springtime of its reign.

Beautiful

The beautiful are beautiful in God
And none but he can see
Their inner worth.
The chapel walls of some poor soul's last agony
Are hung with deeds hidden from worldly view
Good things spoken and words
Ministered like a balm that mended brokenness

And forgiveness too - that friend that came
Before the going down of the sun
And chose to stay past home time
Past prayer time
Past sleep.

Grace

It is grace in full flow
That transports me beyond
My own limitations.
It is grace that dresses me for battle
Against the prevailing winds.

It is grace that gives me vision
To see a situation through eyes
More seeing than my own.

It is grace that bends
My will
To His
And I am smitten.

Redeemer

To believe in the Redeemer
Is to believe in a flock
And a shepherd who cares.

To believe in wisdom
Is to incline towards the will
Of one who knows best.

To believe in hope is to
Place one's hand
With absolute trust
On the door of the day
And enter
Its exquisite liturgy of light.

The Soul

The soul is like sea water
Flowering on the sand;
Petals lapping, overlapping
Bursting
Bubbling
Creating beautiful things
As offerings to the Divine.

The soul is like a vessel
Afloat a green ocean
A woven-sailed
Prayer house
In stillness
And in motion.

Peaceful In His Love

We are rich
Who are clothed
In the garment of righteousness
Woven in truth
At Pentecost.

We are as consuming fire
Like flames on ancient hilltops
We are aglow
Red-robed in sovereignty
Crowned from above
The Spirit rests upon us
Who are peaceful in His love.

The God of Welcomes

…the God of welcomes
Fastens to himself a hope
That none will be lost…

…the endless search goes on
Amid trampled grasses
And sun-forsaken acres
To places of
Thick-walled resistance…

…he extends his call
Love is offered
As word
As hope
As pearl-encrusted
Truth for all…

2nd Sunday

To their locked-in selves
He revealed himself
As the beautiful wound-bearing God.

Their eyes and hearts are opened
As he prays peace on them

He who died
Is risen and
Is as he was
God among men;
But with aspect changed.
All-Heavenly now,
Tabor-light infused,
And when he breathes on them
Love's outpouring of sweetness
Light upon light
They and the Spirit are one.

If Rivers Rebelled Against Us

If rivers rebel against us
And forests uproot their trees
Even if mountains tumble
And rumble down into the sea
God would never give up on us
For he loves us more than these.

If every flower stopped blooming
And all blue skies turned grey
Even if beautiful sunsets
Were stolen clean away
God would never give up on us
For he loves us night and day.

If darkness covers the land
And enemies camp at our door
And doubts and worries assail us
And rattle us right to the core
God would never give up on us
For he loves us more and more.

And the proof of His love
Is the Advocate, gifted to us from above
The power of the Spirit to heal us
And gather us into God's love.

Holy Spirit, Breath of God

Holy Spirit
Breath of God
Breathe on me
Live in me
Pray in me
Guide my steps
Fill my heart
And mind and soul
With your wisdom and love
So that at sunrise and sunset
At midday and in the stillness
Of the night
I may praise
And sanctify and glorify
My life in you
My work in you
My rest in you.

As a flower turns
Towards the new day's light
May I raise my thoughts towards you
And in precious moments of silent devotion
May I listen and be open
To your grace, your prompting.
Ready to forgive when forgiveness
Is called for,

Ready to love for love is the way
Striving
To do the best I can
Each hour
Each day.

Holy Bible Poem

The bible is the alphabet of prayer
The ladder by which we rise
The golden stair.

The bible is the lighthouse on the rocks
A pillar of truth
As telling as gilded hands on clocks
As pleasing to the ear as songs of birds
In spring-winged flocks.

Corpus Christi Poem

Corpus Christi,
Alive in me
A song in my soul
A bell of joy tolling
Liberty! Liberty!

Corpus Christi
In-dwelling guest
How can the world know
Unless I tell them?

How can I tell them unless
I share the goodness of Him
That's in me?
Corpus Christi
Corpus Christi.

His Most Sacred Heart

The chambers of his heart are not plush-lined
As rawness goes they are towards raw inclined
And yet there's sweetness there
That grows as vine
Where grapes of love cascade
As wine sublime.

The chambers of his heart are open wide
And sinners gather there to reconcile
The ragged edges
Of his wounded side
Where flame of
Mercy flows as rolling tide.

The fire that burns within is passion's claim
No greater love there is, nor holier name
Its purest flame
Age to age unfolds
As light divine defines
His heart of gold.

Immaculate Heart of Mary

I stood close by the cleft at Lourdes gazing at
The statue placed where Mary is said to have
stood
And I tried to imagine the scene
As it has been recorded
But nothing came – my mind was blank

And yet my heart raced there
At a level more deep than words
More vivid than imagination
Conversation between a mother
And child took place -
Two hearts, one sullied,
One immaculate.

The Enclosure

Mary's heart is an enclosure, an embrace
In which our weakness
Becomes hallowed in true motherly strength.
Hers is a fostering
That draws us out of ourselves –
And always to a better place.

Ours is the invitation
To the source of her giving
Where grace after grace
Is imparted
Fruited in one
Whose womb bore the Son.

Ours is the need
To linger under the branches of her knowing
Where all that is broken or pained
Can be healed and restored
Through grace
And willingness to love.

Discernment

We often find our worth in silence.
The great task
God has willed for each of us
Can be revealed
Through listening alone.

God's surprise
Is our stumbling upon a
Flowering in the wilderness
When our desire to serve
Appears as much a God-send
As an eternal spring
Washing the face of the earth.

We find our worth
And we give thanks to him.

Passage

The dilution of darkness has begun.
Receive the dawn
Like you would
A true friend.

Open your eyes to
The vista before you

Let grace imprint its dignity on
The whispered word
The open palm
The pendant tears.

Enter into death as
If you were returning
To a homeland you love
The welcome
You were made for.

The Trace of His Love

I do not doubt
That it is God
Who has placed this longing in me.

I do not doubt that my soul was touched
By His hand.

I do not doubt that he breathed on me
Before I was born.

And ever since then
Something within me
That I have come to call grace
Moves me to respond

To the echo
The wave
The trace
Of His Love.

A Holy and Happy Christmas to You

I wish you peace of heart and mind and soul;
I wish you the love of the infant Jesus
And protection in the company of the Blessed
Virgin Mary, St Joseph and the angels.

I wish you the serenity that comes from knowing
That in the birth of Jesus
The world rejoices in what happened long ago,
Enjoys renewal with each unfolding day,
And looks forward in hope to the time
When the Kingdom of God will be fulfilled
And Christ will come again
In all His glory.

Too Soon

Something that resembles night
Takes hold
Stars are shunted out of sight
And the mind starved of reason;
Yet somewhere in that void
The angels are
For they, like God, are everywhere.

He alone knows the final shape of things
The contours of the heart
The way leaves twist and fall
Before they come to rest
He has a finger on the pulse of suffering
And clearing mist
Reveals Love manifest.

Advent

Will He know me at all?
Will I be ready
With everything in place
Or will there be a clutter of plates
Where a space should be
And fogginess where light should be.

Am I skilled in the preparedness
Of one waiting for Christ?
Lead me, Lord, take me where
I need to go
With heart, and eyes
And ears and mind
Open to the gifts
Of the season
Of the coming
Of the Lord.

Snowdrops - The Footsteps of St Brigid

For Sheila O'Brien

The footsteps of St Brigid are everywhere I go
Rising out of darkness from the earth below
Little bells of Spring time -
Pure and white as snow.

The footsteps of St Brigid
Have travelled far and wide
Unconstrained by boundaries,
Monarchies or tides -

An abbess and a foundress
A holy one of God
Whose prayers rose up like incense
From rock and field and bog.

O Saint Brigid, Ireland's children
Still recall with greatest pride
All you did for church and country
With the Cross your truest guide.

Ask the Saviour now to bless us
Ask Our Lady to enfold
In maternal wraps of goodness
All we are and all we hold.

May we follow in your footsteps
As you look from heaven above
May you shower upon your children
Heaven's grace and heaven's love.

To Mountains They Call

To mountains they call,
To the breeze, to night's darkness
And day's light, to caverns they call
And to trees, to depths and valleys and heights

To every place under the sky
To every ear that can hear
The hungry, the hungry cry -
Too dry for the shedding of tears.

*"This poor man cried, and the Lord heard him:
and saved him out of all his troubles."*

Psalm 34:6

In My Father's House

In the early years of our marriage we lived for several years in a small semi which we eventually out-grew. The adjoining house was occupied by an elderly widow, a sincere and affable soul, originally from the country, but settled now in this house bought for her by her sons after she had raised her family. Sadly, after a fall and a spell in hospital the old lady passed away. I missed our little chats over the hedge and after a while I started to have a recurring dream.

It was always the same: I was speaking with her excitedly, explaining how I had discovered a doorway in the kitchen of our home that led to a series of rooms, all empty but very brightly lit – we were both baffled by this since her house and ours were identical in layout. Eventually the dreams stopped and it was some time later before I began to ask myself if our roles in the dreams had somehow been reversed, and was it she who was speaking to me of a house with many mansions?

"In My Father's house there are many mansions. Were it not so, I should have told you, because I go to prepare a place for you. And if I go and prepare a place for you, I am coming

again, and I will take you to Myself; that where I am, there you also may be. And where I go you know, and the way you know."

John 14:1-4

Purity of Intention

Sometimes we do something with the intention of pleasing another and the whole thing is misunderstood. We can find ourselves harshly treated in a circumstance where we might have anticipated joy.

Other times we do something convincing ourselves it is for the good of another when in fact it is a self-serving action – something we hope will elevate us in the eyes of others, or from which we will personally gain.

But God sees through us – and for that alone we ought to be eternally grateful. There's no-one better at helping us remove the veils of self-deception , for God loves us so much we can be assured that anything he ever does is to help us grow in virtue, closer to Him and in conformity to His will – the hand that wounds is the hand that heals.

To know that God sees everything and looks at the heart can then, depending on how you look at it, be an assurance or a caution. It's certainly worth remembering.

*"O Lord, you have searched me and known me.
You know when I sit down and when I rise up;
you discern my thoughts from far away."*

Psalm 139

Simeon and Anna

I've been thinking about Simeon. It's likely
there were some that thought him an old fool,
gone on religion, waiting for something that
wasn't going to happen; a 'holy Joe' who spent
his time in the temple with the likes of Anna
who never seemed to be anywhere else.

Simeon was a man of faith. The moment he had
waited for arrived, and prompted by the Spirit he
and Anna went to the temple to greet Mary and
Joseph and the baby Jesus who was recognised
as the Messiah.

God had not reneged on His promise. Simeon
knew in his heart that when he looked at the
baby Jesus he was looking at the fulfilment of
that promise.

What was true for Simeon is true for us too. God
has promised that the Holy Spirit will be with
the Church until the end of time, and although
we may grow impatient at times with the way
things are, or we may be tempted to find answers
to things beyond our comprehension, perhaps it
is best to be like Simeon. To pray, to wait, to
live in hope that we will one day see God face to
face in the temple of his kingdom.

It's comforting that the beautiful words of
Simeon are uttered still, each and every day in
the universal night prayer of the Church.

Now, Master, you let your servant go in peace.
You have fulfilled your promise.
My own eyes have seen your salvation, which
you have prepared in the sight of all peoples.
A light to bring the Gentiles from darkness; the
glory of your people Israel.

Nunc dimittis

Sweet Trinity and St Patrick

No human cries abound on this bleak hilltop
Only the sound of sheep and wind and wings.
Amid this loneliness, in the absence
Of men's voices I commune with God
And am rapt in mists of wonder -
Never thirsting, never hungering
Beyond the moment I am in
Where God lives and rests in me
And I in Him.

Imitation of Christ

If thinking about God does not move us in heart, head, soul and body, there's a real danger of our religious practice being reduced to nothing but lip service. All we do and say, the way we live our lives should be a continuous outward expression of our well-placed hope in God. It should be obvious to others that we are bearers of good news and followers of Jesus who is *"the way the truth and the life."* (*John 14:6)*

We may have builder's hands coarsened and calloused, we may have bent backs and arthritic joints, we may be unemployed with little or no property but when we know God we have a dignity all our own and we can rest secure in Him and his unchanging ways.

We need not reach up for He has stooped low, we need not go searching for we have been found, we need not feel unloved for we are loved indeed, and we need not ever judge ourselves to be beyond the mercy and forgiveness of Jesus' open arms.

If the gospel of the crucified Christ speaks to us in our hearts, then we will be further moved by compassion when considering the plight of those in our own country and in other lands, crucified on rugged crosses of hunger, addiction or loneliness, casualties of war, disease or rejection. In helping them we are imitating Him by giving a cup of water to the thirsty, bringing comfort to the afflicted.

"But he emptied himself, taking the form of a slave, becoming as human beings are; and being in every way like a human being, he was humbler yet, even to accepting death, death on a cross."

Phil 2:7-8

Prayer to the Holy Spirit

O sweet consoler
Live in me
Help me create for you
The finest dwelling place
Let me furnish it as pleases you
And light it with the truth
That comes from heaven

May you find in my soul
A worthy abode
And may I through you be blessed
With companionship
And guidance
So that I may journey safely
Through this life and into the next
To reach that place prepared for me
In the mansions of eternity.

God's Design

Walk in faith; believe in God
Carry no haversack, no sandals

Journey into the tabernacle of the night
With no less sureness than if it were day

Look to the truth
Not as a rushlight

But as a flaming torch
By which to walk God's way

And treasure those moments -
Few though they are -

That contain enough
For us to know

In temporariness
In fleeting little glimpses
At least

That what lies ahead, beyond,
Is in essence more real
Than could ever be imagined

And holds itself convincingly
As light
As sign

That all -
All is God's design.

Easter Poem 2009

Death has lost its dreaded sting
Christ now reigns as Lord and King
Offering Himself for men
That we, like Him, will rise again.
Alleluia
Alleluia.

Tell and re-tell the amazing story-
Heaven and earth are filled with glory
Victory over death is won and
Eternity is spun
In golden threads
Of the Risen Son.
Alleluia
Alleluia

A Place for You

The exile often dreams of green hills far away. Some might say other hills are just as pleasing to the eye and who would deny it but the thought of one's homeland and the picturing of it in one's mind puts such a personal stamp on things that the stored image retains an incomparability in terms of beauty and longing.

When we think of the life hereafter, the place prepared for us, how do we picture it? We have no memories to draw on, only faith and imagination. And yet, deep within us is the belief that heaven will indeed be beautiful, well beyond our imaginings, and will contain everything our souls could ever yearn for.

Is it possible the exile's longing to return to his homeland is an expression of a deeper-seated yearning within each human soul to return at the end of life's journey to the source from which we came – into the arms of Him who made us, an eternity prepared for us?

"I go to prepare a place for you."

John 14:3

Hope in Heaven

In many ways it is futile to imagine what heaven is like since it is beyond our merely human imaginings, yet I often think how awesomely indescribable a dimension it must be where angels - Cherubim and Seraphim - sing without ceasing. How tired we become of routine, how quickly we grow weary; how soon we are bored, and how readily we look for something new, something different.

And yet in heaven the presence of the unchanging God in all his glory is met with unceasing praise and adoration. Into this scene then and at its centre are Our Lady, our heavenly Mother and Queen, the apostles, and hundreds upon hundreds of the Church's canonised saints.

And there among the great and the good, the patriarchs and matriarchs, the prophets, the early church fathers and the martyrs, are tens of thousands of erstwhile 'ordinary' souls - hidden, uncanonised saints from my family and yours, as well as beggars of yore, the disabled, the sick and afflicted, the persecuted and the blind, all come to perfection now and united with the Father, Son, and Holy Spirit. These purified souls are enjoying the reward of the beatific vision and the peace of Christ in the light of their heavenly home. Therein rests the hope of the suffering world.

Witness

When we attend church and become involved in different ways in parish life we can then at least do what Thomas did – we can reach out and feel the presence of Christ, we can place ourselves where we need to be placed in order to be spiritually invigorated, renewed. It does us far more good at times to get out of ourselves and be inspired by the witness of others. And then of course for others the opposite is true.

It will be through our witness that they will receive the grace and the courage to become witnesses too, having placed their hand in the side of the wounded Christ, having felt the pulse of the mystical body; they too will become invigorated, renewed.

"Then he spoke to Thomas, 'Put your finger here; look, here are my hands. Give me your hand; put it into my side. Do not be unbelieving

any more but believe.' Thomas replied, 'My Lord and my God!'"

John 20: 27-28

Month of May

Just now when so much of nature is saying yes to God, we are mindful of Our Lady in this lovely month of May. Every bluebell is a bell that sounds the Ave, every hedgerow bears a blossom for her hair, every Angelus reminds us of the story of the angel and of how Mary listened in prayerful humility.

In her youthfulness and simplicity Mary complied entirely with the will of God and carried within her virgin womb through the overshadowing of the Holy Spirit, the Word Incarnate, he who was the son of God made man.

We too can follow Mary's example, and carry Jesus into the world, visiting those places where there is hunger and blindness and despair, we can bring the love of the Lord into the lives of those around us in a truly meaningful way while sustaining ourselves through prayer and the Eucharist.

In imitation of Our Lady, we too must learn to become listeners and bearers as we bend to the will of God, forsaking our own will for what is better, for God knows best.

Mary

The story of Mary is a sorrowful mystery and a joyful mystery that ends in glory. No human being will ever be called to do what Mary did – yet her uniqueness does not alienate but rather it draws us to her heart and the heart of her Son as we follow the worldly path she once walked, carrying Christ's light with us and in us wherever we go.

The beauty of Mary is that of pure goodness. In iconic writings her arms hold the baby Jesus in such a tender embrace that we are at once convinced of her motherliness as she looks attentively towards us with tender eyes of love and mercy. The enormity of the truth that we are her children can be difficult to take in at first -

and Mary's greatest desire as our Mother is to pour upon us the graces given her by God.

She is that flower most fair, that sweetness and tenderness whose life and virtues we strive to imitate, the Immaculate Heart whose purity knows no blemish or stain. Through the pain and darkness of Calvary Mary stood steadfast as a rock alongside her suffering Son and accepted from him in his dying breath the gift of all of us – adopting us as her own, as sisters and brothers in Him. And we, too, turn to Mary as heaven's gift and advocate, our proven hope in adversity, the bright star of the heavens and motherly source of solace and joy.

Lourdes

Even for those who wish to lend no credence to the actual visitation of Our Lady to Bernadette at Lourdes, there is still much to be said for it as a place of prayer and overwhelming peace.

Here the universal church is well represented and nothing draws the eye more than the sight of the sick and afflicted - the church suffering.

Caught up in the midst of their suffering is beauty - real beauty of heart and soul, of mind and intellect and as one processes along the boulevard during the candlelight procession, led by the sick and suffering and all those who come to serve them, it is a most humbling experience to see those candles burning – each one representing a human life, a soul that bears within it the light of Christ. And as each candle is raised higher at each Ave chorus our hearts and minds too are lifted up.

The Standard Rose

In the silence that descends
After the great amen
There is
The miracle of the rose -
Neither seen nor scented,
But perfectly composed.

It has a bearing
All its own
And occupies its space
In mood sedate and elegant
Among the commonplace

And in the morning
Bright and full
Its yellow blooms proclaim
The wellness of its being
The aptness of its name.

Eucharist

Sometimes we can feel small, like a little grain of sand on a beach and yet we are not small. We, when assimilated into Christ's body, are anything but small. What wonders can be worked in us, what goodness can flow like streams through the darkness of the world, what lights we carry, what lights we become when assimilated into that one light that gives Himself to us in the Eucharist, for the life of the world!

Jesus said to the Jews:

"I am the living bread which has come down from heaven. Anyone who eats this bread will live forever; and the bread that I shall give is my flesh, for the life of the world."

John 6:51-52

Assumption of the Blessed Virgin Mary (1)

Surely none would begrudge you a throne
And angels around
Or begrudge you a crown,
For you, O Mary, did bear such a cross
Of sevenfold sorrow that ended with
The loss
Of your dear son,
The Lord God Jesus Christ upon a cross.
Dear Heaven is your home now,
Fairest One,
There, stars form a crown about your head
And angels around you sing -
The same that carried you from your bed
And laid your head on wings
That also spread to form
Down on which to lie
Safe-journeying your sacred body
High, heavenward
Where you reign as Queen
Mother of God
Mother of mercy
In reign supreme.

Assumption (2)

Your eyes opened to a new kind of light
Wide pools that gaze with merciful love upon
the world
Your sword-pierced heart, immaculate,
Strong-walled as a cathedral
In the holy city of God.

Angels surround your throne
Heralds of assumption, of queenship,
Holy Blessed Virgin,
Mother of God
Star-crowned Queen of heaven
Queen of angels

We, though sinners, are yours,
Every tribe on earth, every race
Beckoned to enclosure
In deep mantle-folds of grace.

Who Do You Say I Am?

In the blessed lonely stillness of the night
When neither darkness nor sleep provide
A safehouse for those who would hide
From truth's confrontational guise:
Who do you say I am?

In the maddening rush of the day
When worlds spin and nerves squeal
When big names play big games
And war's lasting image of all that's gone wrong
Is a tiny left footprint
In a blood-muddied field:
Who do you say I am?

In the unfathomable reaches of the sea
Where no earthly spirit can dwell
Myth and mystery and meaning
Wash over swell upon swell
Then out of the blue a whisper
Like a beacon of light in a storm
The question that echoes down centuries:
Who do you say I am?

Amid tyranny, murder and outrage
Avarice, betrayal and war
The enduring words of the Master forge
The same keen edge as before

Cutting through masks of deceivers
Through evil, corruption and sham
The question as probing as ever:
Who do you say I am?

Name Above All Names

It is not obedience or goodness or holiness that
brings us to God but rather an awareness of our
disobedience, sin, and indifference that moves us
to pray that, one day, through perseverance and
grace we may become all we ought to be as heirs
to a kingdom and children born of light.

Like the finding of water in parched and barren
land or a sudden sprouting of wild flowers in a
desolate landscape, God is full of surprises.

To find God is to find treasure beyond
imagining. In Him we can place our whole trust,
our past, present and future as He reaches out to
us in boundless mercy and love.

In finding God we can sustain others and support
ourselves, for God is like the great oak tree
which shelters us his children beneath its wide-
spread branches - the extensions of his love.

God is the soundness of ground beneath our feet, the wellspring of hope, the dream that becomes reality, and the name that is above all names.

In finding God, in offering our lives to Him, we become liberated beyond words, freed from prisons and snares and quagmires of the past, from slavery and corruption of the present, our eyes and hearts are opened anew as we begin to view the world and all that is in it through the windows of his eyes.

Penitential

When I look at the dazzling whiteness of swans gliding across murky water I am reminded of sin and grace, how swans can exist day after day uncontaminated by the waters they occupy, just as we can learn the secret of surviving in a world polluted by the evil of sin and the darkness of despair.

New Year's Day 2005

Foul weather marked the start of it –
Where winds cut through fallow fields
Grasses bent
Like worshippers of an unseen god.

Snapped branched lay strewn on roads
Obstacles for the few
Who ventured beyond their own soil.

The cold hand of January had extended itself
But the lure of the fireside proved strong
Civility was put on hold
As doors closed and rain drops spilled
Diamond after diamond on the firs.

Hail, O Cross, Our Only Hope

There really is only one choice to be made in life – either we embrace the cross or we rail against it. All other choices, all other areas of life are affected and permeated by this first and most important choice. Whether we like it or not, the cross is part of our lives - run away and it will follow, try to exchange it for another and find you're worse off than before, but embrace it and you'll enter into a peacefulness that will bring meaning to your life, labour and love – such is this saintly embrace.

The cross can become for you a powerful symbol of hope. It can be an assurance - the only true one - that bridges the gap between this life and the next. We can look at the cross and say – 'Here is my brother, Lord Jesus, who died that I might live, who rose from the dead so as to do away with death, who ascended to heaven to show me the way.'

A beautiful story is written in the wounds of the Saviour, such a heart-rending tale is there for the telling – over and over and over again. Embrace the cross, do not be afraid – it will be the making of you. Stand at the cross as did the faithful two – be one with them in a world of the misunderstood.

Manifestation

For Fr Tom Kiggins

We are like children who sleep out under the
stars
Protected by a blanket of faith
Our gazing upward is instinctive
As our eyes trace the pattern of paths
Across the heavens
And we know that as the wind blows east and
west
North and south
The dust from desert sands is swirling
somewhere still
As the breath of his knowing falls
As droplets
On green hills.

I Lean On the Rose of Mary

I lean on the rose of Mary
The flower of heaven
And Queen of Angels.

No face is fairer
No woman's soul more holy

In her loving way
She reposes over the fallen world
And offers the grace of knowing

That delivers us to God.

Notes

- -

- -

- -

- -

- -

- -

- -

- -

All proceeds from this book will go to charity.